HARCOURT SOCIAL Studies

Social Studies in Action

Resources for the Classroom

Grade 2

Harcourt

SCHOOL PUBLISHERS

www.harcourtschool.com

ISBN-13: 9780153494192
ISBN-10: 0-15-349419-0

1 2 3 4 5 6 7 8 9 10 054 16 15 14 13 12 11 10 09 08 07

Contents

Introduction

This *Social Studies in Action: Resources for the Classroom* booklet provides a variety of activities designed to help teachers facilitate and spark social studies learning in the classroom through fun hands-on projects or skill pages. Some of these activities require children to imagine they live in another time, while others will prompt children to write creatively about how character, economic, or citizenship issues relate to their lives. All the included projects, activities, geography questions, drama activities, and games will help children gain a better understanding of important social studies content. The following kinds of activities are included.

Bag Ladies Activity   These activities provide children with hands-on art projects that will help them connect with social studies content in an imaginative and fun way. Only common art supplies or household items, such as brown paper bags, are required to complete the activities.

Drama Activity   These readers theatres will get children excited about social studies content by asking them to participate in an engaging storyline or tale set in the past or present.

Simulations and Games   Simulations help children gain a better understanding of social studies content by asking them to assume the role of an individual involved in a historical or contemporary situation. Games give children the chance to explore history, economics, and other social studies content in a challenging but fun and interactive manner.

Long-Term Project   These month-long projects are designed to promote cooperation as children work together to produce a presentation or artistic creation related to social studies content. Each project is divided into four sessions, and a session is completed per week.

Short-Term Projects   These projects will help children explore social studies content by singing songs, drawing pictures, making models, and so on.

Writing Projects   These writing prompts will help children use and improve their writing skills as they explore social studies content and issues.

Daily Geography   This section provides grade-appropriate questions designed to help children learn or review geography facts.

Why Character Counts   Each of these activities focuses on an important character trait. Children read about each trait and complete a hands-on activity to reinforce understanding.

Economic Literacy   Children learn about important economic concepts and complete an activity on sound economics. Often, these activities ask children to apply economic concepts to a scenario or choice.

Citizenship   This feature is divided into three sections. Children learn about various citizenship concepts such as freedoms granted by the Bill of Rights, equality, government, and voting. Children enrich their understanding of these concepts by participating in a teacher-led discussion and by completing writing activities that ask them to reflect on how citizenship concepts affect their lives.

Stars and Stripes Quarterly

Unit I

Materials needed:

*Drawing paper

*Colored pencils

*Tempera paint

*Brushes

*Water

*Brush clean-up cups

*Pencil and black marker

*Notebook paper

*Stapler

Social Studies Skills:

*Picture Graphs

*Choosing a Leader

Reading Skills:

*Generalize

*Point of View

*Main Idea and Details

Instructions:

1. Create and decorate the title area of the magazine.

2. Draw a self-portrait under the title and color it in with colored pencils or paint. When the portrait is dry, outline it with the black marker.

Illustrations:

3. Write to this prompt: "I would make a good leader in my classroom because . . ."

4. Include details about why you would make a good leader by using the topics from the chapter.

5. After editing your story, make a clean copy or use the computer to type it. The stories are then stapled to the magazine cover.

6. You may want to add a second page with a picture graph that relates to the magazine article.

A Student Government Team

A readers theatre play about running for student government

Cast of Characters

- Narrator
- Teacher
- Marco Sanchez
- Jessie Brill
- Claire Johnson
- Susan Arnold
- Brian Tran

Narrator: After lunch, the students of Room 12 return to their classroom.

Teacher: Listen up, class. I want each of you to imagine you are running for student government. Each of you will make a poster. What do you think your poster should say?

Marco: It should have your name in big, bold letters so people know who to vote for!

Claire: People also need to know what you are running for.

Susan: Your posters should have sayings or pictures.

Teacher: Those are all good ideas. Go ahead and get started.

Narrator: The students move into groups and start their work. One group is made up of Marco, Jessie, Claire, Brian, and Susan.

Marco: Jessie, what are you going to run for?

Jessie: I want to be mayor. That way I can tell everyone else what to do.

Claire: A mayor is the leader of a city. A student president runs the student government. But I don't think the student president gets to tell people what to do.

Marco: Well, I am going to run for king.

Susan: People don't run for king! You're either born a king or you're not. Kings and queens are born into families that are part of the government.

Marco: Oh, all right. I will run for president. But I still think King Marco sounds good.

Claire: I want to run for treasurer. Treasurers are in charge of money.

Jessie: That makes sense. You are good at math. I don't know what to run for.

Susan: Check this out.

Narrator: Susan holds up a poster that reads, "Susan for Judge: Break the Rules, You're Out of School."

Jessie: Wow, good thing there is no judge on student council.

Susan: Did I get something wrong? What do judges do?

Brian: Judges make sure the laws are fair for everyone.

Jessie: It is a good thing the principal is in charge of that.

Brian: Why don't you run for sports commissioner, Susan?

Susan: That sounds like a good idea. I like sports.

Marco: Hey, I have an idea. The parts of government work together to get things done. Let's be a team. Our posters can show how we are a team.

Claire: Yes! This way we can help each other. Marco, you already want to be president.

Jessie: And I'll be vice president. Claire is treasurer. Susan is sports commissioner. Brian, that leaves you.

Brian: Our team doesn't have a secretary. I will run for that. Besides, I'm a good writer.

Claire: And you are organized. I bet that helps.

Marco: Sounds good. Okay, as your president, I am suggesting that we get busy. Notice how I didn't just boss you around?

Brian: Yeah. I might actually vote for you. Come on, we don't have much more time.

Narrator: The group gets busy writing and drawing their posters. Twenty minutes pass by.

Teacher: Okay, time is up. Groups, finish what you are doing on your posters. Get ready to share.

Narrator: Several students share their posters. Then the teacher calls on Marco.

Teacher: Marco, would you like to share your poster?

Marco: Sure, but I am not alone. I am running for student government with a team.

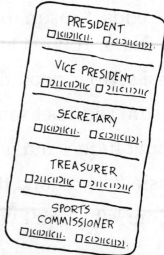

Narrator: Marco, Jessie, Claire, Susan, and Brian all walk up to the front of the room carrying their posters.

Marco: I am Marco Sanchez. As president, I will lead our school wisely.

Jessie: I am Jessie Brill. I am running for vice president. I will be responsible and fair.

Claire: Vote for me, Claire Johnson. As treasurer, I will carefully watch where our money goes.

Susan: My name is Susan Arnold. I am running for sports commissioner. I will work to get new balls for our school.

Brian: Vote for me, Brian Tran, for secretary. I'll make sure our meetings go well.

All students: Vote for us, and we will work together as a team for you!

THE END

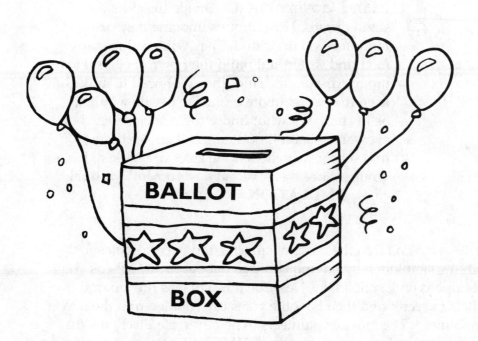

Simulations and Games

Democracy Dominoes Have children create word dominoes by dividing index cards into two parts. On one half, ask them to write the name of a person in government such as *President, mayor, governor, council member, judge,* or *citizen.* On the other half, ask them to write a vocabulary word, job, or place related to the government such as *state capital, Congress, White House, justice, law, court, city council, rights,* or *consequence.* Playing in small groups, have the first child put down a domino and tell how the two words on the domino are related. After that, players take turns adding dominoes by placing one end of a domino next to a related word on the chain. Each player explains how the words are related. Play continues until all matches have been made. **GAME**

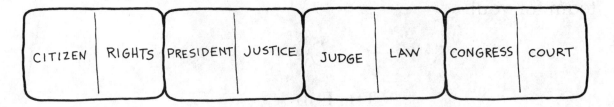

| CITIZEN | RIGHTS | PRESIDENT | JUSTICE | JUDGE | LAW | CONGRESS | COURT |

Island Government Divide the class into small groups. Have groups imagine they are marooned on an island. They will need to collect food and water and build their own shelters. Have groups discuss the rules they will need to make to keep the peace. Invite groups to decide who will be in charge of what and write a set of rules that everyone must follow. Remind them to discuss and set consequences if the rules are broken. Have groups share their "island government" with the class. **SIMULATION**

Voting Day Assign children the parts of citizens and of candidates for President. Begin the simulation by having children act out their parts as you narrate what happens on Election Day. Describe how citizens line up and mark their ballots in secret and then how the votes are counted and the new President is announced. Then invite volunteers to help narrate Election Day role-plays for electing a governor and a mayor. **SIMULATION**

Press Conference Invite children to role-play a press conference about the government. Explain that at a press conference, someone gives radio, television, and newspaper reporters information about something important. At this press conference, govenment leaders will talk about their roles and responsibilities. Assign half of the class to be government leaders and half to be reporters for the different media. Provide children with index cards. Ask the government leaders to write short paragraphs on their cards explaining their roles. The reporters will take notes on their cards as the leaders read their paragraphs aloud during the conference. Then the reporters may question the leaders. After the conference, have the reporters summarize the leaders' speeches from their notes, as if reporting the news. **SIMULATION**

Make a Pair Write each of the following people and jobs on separate index cards:

President	Carries out laws of the country
Governor	Carries out laws of the state
Mayor	Carries out laws of the city
Congress	Makes laws of the country
State legislature	Makes laws of the state
City council	Makes laws of the city
Supreme Court	Checks fairness of the country's laws
State courts	Checks fairness of the state's laws
City courts	Checks fairness of the city's laws

Have groups of children place all cards face down and take turns flipping over two cards at a time. If the cards match, the player keeps the pair. The player with the most pairs wins. **GAME**

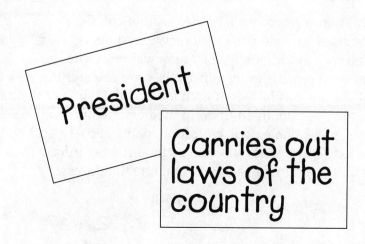

President

Carries out laws of the country

UNIT 1 Long-Term Project

A LOCAL GOVERNMENT DIRECTORY

Use this project to help children understand the roles and responsibilities of their local government officials.

Week 1   Introduce
 group   30 minutes

Materials: paper, pencils

Introduce this project by discussing the structure of the local government in your city or town. Discuss the roles of local officials by asking the following questions: Who are the elected officials in our city government? What do the elected officials do at City Hall? Why are the jobs they do important to the community?

To get the discussion started, you can ask children if they or their parents have ever seen a city council meeting in person or on a local cable television channel.

Explain to children that they are going to create a directory of local city government officials. Divide children into groups, and have each group compile a list of local officials. Remind children that some officials are elected by citizens, and other officials are appointed. To help children get started, you may want to suggest some titles of officials, such as *mayor, city council member, sheriff, judge.*

Week 2   Plan
 group   45 minutes

Materials: paper, pencils, research materials

Have children research each of the positions on their list. Encourage them to use the library, newspapers, or the Internet. Additionally, they may want to write  letters or send e-mails to the offices they are researching. Ask children to find out the responsibilities of each job and the name of the person currently holding the position. In addition to the person's name, students might include the person's age, hometown, education, political party, and number of years in the position. Children should also include contact information for the person, such as a phone number, address, and e-mail address.

Week 3 Construct

 group  45 minutes

Materials: drawing paper, crayons or markers, construction paper, glue or tape, hole punch, yarn

Have children put together their directory. Ask them to create a page for each position they researched. They may wish to include photos or drawings of the officials or of the buildings the officials work in, along with the information gathered during Week 2. Have each group bind the directory between two sheets of construction paper and add a title and decorations to the cover.

Week 4 Present

 group  15 minutes

Materials: display area for directories, camera (optional)

Have the groups place their directories on a table or a group of desks. Invite children to explore the directories made by their classmates. If possible, take a picture of each directory surrounded by the children who made it.

Tips for Combination Classrooms

 For Grade 1 Students: Have children include a section in the directory explaining how community leaders help people.

 For Grade 3 Students: Have children include a section in the directory explaining the structure of local, state, and national government in the United States.

Short-Term Projects

Use these projects to help children explore citizenship and government.

In the News
 partners 30 minutes

Materials: newspapers, news magazines, posterboard, scissors, tape or glue

Ask children to create a chart on a sheet of posterboard with the following headings: *The President, The Congress, The Supreme Court.* Then ask children to look through newspapers and news magazines for photos and reports of our government at work. Have children clip these photos and reports and tape or glue each under the appropriate column heading.

Successful Student Rule Book
group 45 minutes

Materials: drawing paper, crayons or markers, construction paper, hole punch, yarn

Have small groups of children brainstorm and list rules that help them be successful students. Remind them that the rules can apply to schoolwork, getting along with others, or being safe. Have each group member choose a rule, write it on a sheet of paper, and draw an illustration for it. Suggest they describe situations when the rule might come in handy. Ask groups to bind their rule pages between two sheets of construction paper to make a book. Have them decorate and title the cover, list their names as authors, and display the book in the class library.

Our Government at Work

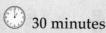 group  30 minutes

Materials: posterboard, crayons or markers, scissors, newspapers and magazines, glue

Invite children to make posters that show how the government is working to help people. Suggest they find and cut out newspaper or magazine articles that tell about a law, project, or community activity. Examples could be a new bike helmet law, a new recreation center, or a city-sponsored art exhibit. Invite children to draw an illustration to accompany the article that shows people benefiting from the law, event, or project. Ask them to create a poster by gluing the article and illustration to posterboard and displaying it in the classroom.

Presidential Trading Cards

 partners 30 minutes

Materials: research materials, drawing paper, crayons or markers

Have children work in pairs to create Presidential Trading Cards. Ask each pair of children to choose a President to research. Then, have them create their own trading card by drawing a picture of their President on the front and listing some facts about him on the back. The facts might include the President's name, birth and death dates, home state, years in office, and any major accomplishments. When children are finished, have them share their cards with the rest of the class.

UNIT **1**

Writing Projects

Our government is made up of citizens who work together to benefit all the people. Use these prompts to get children writing about their role in government.

Election Night Speech

 individual  30 minutes

Ask children to pretend that they have just been elected to represent your state in Congress. Ask them to write a short speech of at least three sentences that explains how they plan to help your state when they get to Washington, D.C. Encourage children to also include what they might do to improve life in your state or community. Ask children who feel comfortable to share their speech with the class.

Groups and Leaders

 individual 20 minutes

Ask children to list all the groups they belong to, including family, class, school, clubs, sports teams, community, state, and the United States. Then have children write the name of the group and its leader next to each entry on their list.

Dear City Council

 individual 30 minutes

Explain to children that each government office has a budget, or a set amount of money, to spend each year. Tell them to imagine that the city council must choose between spending the money on a community pool or a new park. Have them write a letter to the city council, telling which would be their choice and why.

Laws and Consequences

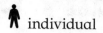 individual  30 minutes

Remind children that laws are rules citizens must follow. If we do not follow the law, there can be consequences. Ask children to brainstorm some of the laws they follow every day. Ask children to write a law they think is important to follow such as wearing a seatbelt when in a car. Then have them write consequences related to the law. For example, they may say if they don't wear a seatbelt, they could be hurt in an accident. If they do follow the law, their parents won't get a ticket.

Choose by Voting

 group  30 minutes

Ask groups of children to use voting to make a choice about a classroom activity, a playground game, a cafeteria food choice, or an assembly. Have each group create a ballot to decide on a choice. For example, if they want classmates to vote on an assembly, they may give choices for a musical group, a sports celebrity, or a movie. Suggest groups establish a way to distribute and collect the ballots. After tallying the ballots, have groups write a report that tells how many people they polled, the number of votes for each choice, and the final results.

Daily Geography

1. **Location** — What are the four main directions?

2. **Regions** — How many states are there in the United States?

3. **Location** — What is the name of your state?

4. **Movement** — Imagine that you and your family will go from Kansas to Oregon. In which direction will you travel?

5. **Regions** — The United States is made up of 50 parts. What are these parts called?

6. **Location** — Which states touch California to the east?

7. **Location** — Which state touches Illinois to the north?

8. **Place** — What do we call a city in which the government of a state meets?

9. **Location** — Which states touch South Dakota to the east?

10. **Location** — Which country does Arizona touch to the south?

11. **Location** — Which state touches Arkansas to the north?

12. **Human-Environment Interactions** — In which state could you see the Pacific Ocean?
Virginia
Illinois
Washington

13. **Location** — Which large body of water does the United States touch to the west?

14. **Location** — Which large body of water does the United States touch to the east?

15. **Movement** — Imagine that you and your family will go from Nevada to North Carolina for a family reunion. In which direction will you travel?

16. Regions Which of these states is in the northern part of the United States?
Michigan
Florida
New Mexico

17. Regions Which of these cities is not located in the western part of the United States?
Portland, Oregon
San Diego, California
El Paso, Texas

18. Regions Which of these cities is located in the southern part of the United States?
Columbus, Ohio
Albany, New York
Austin, Texas

19. Human-Environment Interactions In which of these cities in the United States could you see boats docked beside the ocean?
El Paso, Texas
Boulder, Colorado
San Diego, California

20. Movement Through which states would you travel going in a straight line from Maine to Connecticut?

21. Movement Through which states would you travel going from Texas to Florida?

22. Location What is the name of our country?

23. Place What are the names of the seven continents?

24. Place On which continent do you live?

25. Place Which two oceans does North America touch?

26. Location Which continent is directly west of North America?

27. Location Which ocean is east of Asia and west of North America?

28. Location On which continent is China?

29. Movement Imagine that you and your family go from China to North America. In which direction will you travel?

30. Location Which state is in the middle of the Pacific Ocean?

Why Character Counts

Fairness

Fairness describes when something is done in a way that is right and honest. It is important that laws treat people with fairness. This means that the law treats everyone equally.

- Trustworthiness
- Respect
- Responsibility
- ✓ **Fairness**
- Caring
- Patriotism

People in history fought for fair laws. Dr. Martin Luther King, Jr., worked to get equal treatment for all Americans. Susan B. Anthony worked to help women get the right to vote.

People today continue to work for fair laws. Judges in courts decide if laws are fair.

In Your Own Words:

When does a law or rule show fairness?

_____

_____

_____

Name _____

～ Activity ～

1. Describe a rule your class has made so everyone is treated fairly.

_____

_____

_____

2. Imagine you and your classmates are playing a ball game on the playground. Several students begin to argue about the rules. What can you all do so that the rules are fair to everyone?

_____

_____

_____

3. Write about a time when something happened to you or another person that you did not think was fair. Why did you think it was not fair? What would you like to do or change so that this situation was fair to everyone?

_____

_____

_____

_____

UNIT 1 Economic Literacy

Services and Volunteers

Some people have jobs that provide a service. They do work for other people for money.

Sometimes people give a service to others without wanting to be paid. Volunteers are people who give their time and service without getting paid for it. Volunteers help other people or groups save money. By giving their time, volunteers help their community.

Mr. Lawrence is a teacher. He gets paid to provide a service to his students. Mr. Lawrence also loves to read. When he heard adults in his community were having trouble reading, he wanted to help. How can Mr. Lawrence volunteer to help others?

Mr. Lawrence volunteers at the local library to teach adults to read better.

Name _____

Try It

Do these problems.

1. Alicia Torres is an artist. She sells many paintings. Alicia noticed that the sign that welcomes people as they drive into town is very old and hard to read. The city does not have the money to pay for a new sign. Which service can Alicia volunteer? How will this service help the city?

_____

_____

2. Dr. Walker is a dentist. He takes care of people's teeth at his office. Dr. Walker read a story in the newspaper about children whose families are very poor. They do not have the money to go to a dentist. What service can Dr. Walker volunteer? How will it help others?

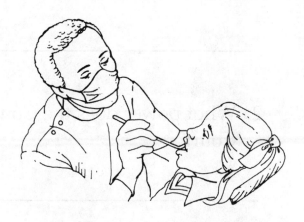

_____

_____

_____

▶ **Read About It**   The Constitution is our country's most important document. It tells how our government is set up. One part gives Congress the power to make laws. Another part gives the President the power to carry out laws. A third part gives the Supreme Court the power to decide if laws are fair. Each year on September 17, people celebrate Constitution Day. This holiday reminds people of how important the Constitution is.

1. Why is the Constitution important to our country?

_____

_____

2. What power does the Constitution give to the Supreme Court?

_____

_____

_____

▶ **Talk About It**   The Constitution describes in writing how our government should work. Why is it important that this is written down?

Name _____

Write About It The Constitution helps Congress, the
President, and the Supreme Court work together to make new
laws. Why is cooperation important? Write about a time you
cooperated with someone else in making a decision.

_____

_____

_____

_____

_____

_____

_____

_____

_____

_____

Land and Water Step Book
Unit 2

Materials needed:

*Construction paper cut in the following way: yellow, 9" x 4"; green, 9" x 6"; blue, 9" x 8"; brown, 9" x 10"; and white, 9" x 12"
*Brown paper grocery bag
*Paper plate
*Crayons
*Watercolors
*Scissors
*Glue
*Labels

Social Studies Skills:

*Land and Water
*Natural Resources
*Environments

Reading Skills:

*Sequence
*Categorize
*Compare and Contrast

Instructions:

1. Cut the construction paper. Stack the colored strips with the shortest on top and the longest on the bottom. Staple the stack to the flap of the bag, creating a step book.

2. Using a green crayon, make landmasses on the paper plate, coloring darkly. Paint the rest of the plate blue. Cut the plate in half, and glue one-half to the bottom flap of the bag.

Illustrations:

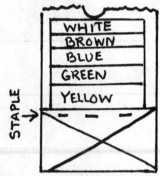

3. Label the layers of the step book for the different environments: Yellow-Desert; Green-Forest; Blue-Water; Brown-Mountains; White-Arctic. Glue a title to the bottom flap, and a label to each of the layers.

4. Cut or decorate the top edge of each layer. Add details such as sand for the desert, glitter for the Arctic, waves for the water, peaks for the mountains, and trees and grass for the forest.

5. Use the bag to store vocabulary, mapwork, and other activities.

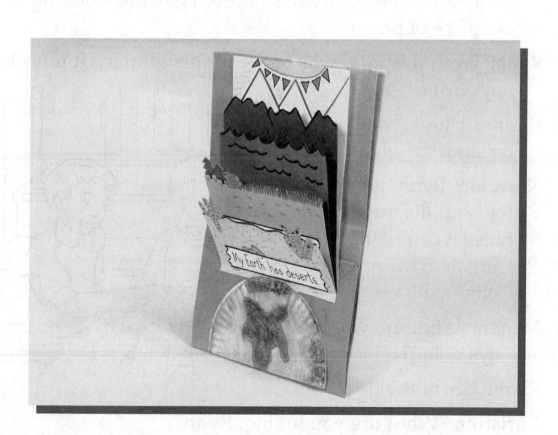

A Secret Map

A readers theatre play about the land and maps

Cast of Characters

- Narrator
- Ryan, age 8
- Christina, Ryan's 10-year-old sister
- Colby, age 8
- Jimmy, Ryan's best friend, age 8
- Megan, age 7

Narrator: On a cool day in September, Jimmy and Ryan sit on the front step of Ryan's house. They are studying an old piece of paper.

Ryan: Wow, this map was really hidden, Jimmy. It must be important.

Jimmy: Uh-oh, someone is coming.

Narrator: Ryan quickly folds up the paper and hides it behind his back. Christina, Megan, and Colby walk up.

Megan: What are you guys doing?

Ryan: Uh, nothing.

Christina: What are you hiding, Ryan?

Ryan: Okay, I'll show you, but you have to promise to keep it a secret.

Narrator: Ryan holds the map out in front of him. The other children look on curiously. The paper is heavy and old. It is covered with odd markings.

Megan: What is it?

Colby: Hey, it's a map. Wow, it's old! I think it marks where someone has hidden something. Maybe it is a treasure!

Jimmy: That's what we thought.

Christina: What makes you think the map will lead to treasure?

Ryan: See these symbols? I think they mark places around our neighborhood. And do you see this?

Colby: I bet that little X with the exclamation point is where the treasure is!

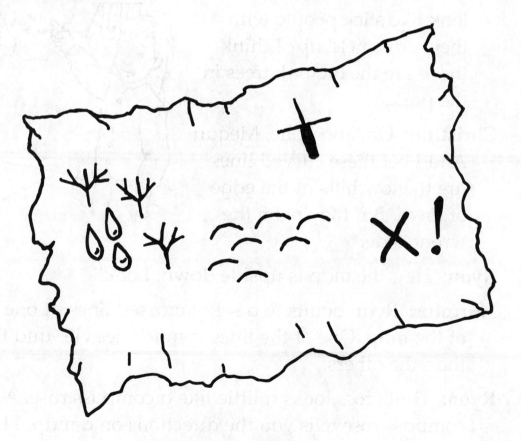

Christina: Ryan, just where did you find this map?

Ryan: Remember that old dresser Mom got at the garage sale last summer? This paper fell out when I opened a drawer.

Colby: So where do we start?

Jimmy: Let's figure out some of these symbols.

Narrator: The children gather around to study the map. Colby pulls out a piece of crumpled paper and a stubby pencil from his pocket.

Colby: I'll make a map key. It's sort of like figuring out a code!

Ryan: Look at these shapes that look like drops of water. I think those might be the old well. It's been here forever!

Megan: And these things that look like stick people with their arms held up? I think those are the big oak trees in the park.

Christina: Oh, good one, Megan. And I bet these curved lines are the low hills at the edge of town. But they're on the wrong side.

Ryan: Hey, the map is upside down. Look!

Narrator: Ryan points to a set of crossed lines at one edge of the map. One of the lines is much heavier and thicker than the others.

Ryan: That cross looks a little like a compass rose. A compass rose tells you the directions on a map. I bet that heavy line points north.

Megan: Why didn't they just mark north with a big N, like other maps?

Jimmy: Because it was meant to trick us!

Colby: Yes, because it is a treasure map!

Christina: You know what else this map needs? Something that tells us how far apart these symbols are.

Jimmy: You're right. Look at how close together the trees and the well are. Then look at how far away the X is! It would take us all day to walk there.

Megan: Let's get our parents to drive us.

Jimmy: Then they would know about the treasure. And how many people would that be?

Christina: Oh come on, Jimmy. If there really is treasure, do you think we would be able to hide it from our parents anyway?

THE END

UNIT 2 Simulations and Games

How Do I Get There From Here? Pair each child with a partner.
Give each pair a map of the United States. Have the children take turns
pretending to be the navigator and the traveler. Have the "traveler" to ask
for directions to a location in the country, such as *How do I get to North
Carolina?*" Invite the "navigator" to explain the route from your state to
the requested location using the map and appropriate directional terms.
Encourage children to take turns playing both roles and finding several
locations. **SIMULATION**

Landform Tag On the playground or gym floor, draw six large circles
and label them *plains, mountain, ocean, island, peninsula,* and *river.* Choose one
child to be IT in the center. Have the other children choose one landform
or body of water and stand inside that circle. Then describe one place,
for example: *If you are standing in a large body of water with whales and sharks
swimming around ships that are passing by, run to a new place.* All the children who
are standing in the circle labeled *ocean* must then run to another circle before
IT tags them. Those who are tagged become IT's helpers. Continue until only
one child remains. That child can be IT for the next game. **GAME**

Where Is It?

Play a game using the whole classroom as the "game board." Label the front of the room *North;* the back, *South;* the left, *West;* and the right, *East.* Have one child leave the room, and while that child is gone, have another hide a beanbag or another object somewhere in the room. Then have the absent child come back in and try to find the object while the other children give directions to it. Have children take turns hiding the object, giving directions, and locating the object. **GAME**

Crazy Locations

Prepare sets of four cards that relate to the unit, such as:

- mountain, hill, plain, valley
- river, ocean, lake, pond
- north, south, east, west
- compass rose, map key, map title, symbols
- Canada, United States, Mexico, Greenland
- suburban, urban, rural, desert

Divide the children into small groups. Invite children to use the cards to play a game in which they draw and discard cards to make a match. Each player is dealt six cards, and the remainder is placed in a draw pile. The top card is turned face up. Children take turns drawing a card from either the player on the left or the draw pile. When they complete a set of four cards, they lay down the set. Play continues until all sets are formed or there are no more cards to draw. **GAME**

Seasons Charades

Create slips of paper with different seasons, climates, and weather conditions written on them, and place them in a container. Have each child draw a slip and think of the activities that are associated with the season, climate, or weather condition. Then have children take turns acting out their activities for the other children to guess. **GAME**

UNIT 2 Long-Term Project

3-D MAPS OF THE LAND

Use this project to help children understand maps and the land around them.

Week 1 Introduce

 group   30 minutes

Materials: large sheets of cardboard, paper, pencils

Introduce the project by asking, "If you were a bird flying over the land, what kinds of things would you see?" Explain that children will work in groups to construct a 3-D map of the land. This map can be imaginary but needs to include examples of landforms, bodies of water, and buildings.

Divide the class into groups. Provide each group with a large piece of cardboard that will be the work surface for the map. Explain that this is the "land" they will work on. Invite groups to discuss what their map will show.

Week 2 Plan

 group   30 minutes

Materials: craft paper, pencils, modeling clay, paint, assorted toys, recycled materials

Encourage groups to begin planning how they will construct their 3-D map. Explain that they can use craft supplies, modeling clay, paint, and assorted toys and recycled bits to construct their map. First, have each group use a piece of craft paper the same size as their cardboard to map out where features will be placed. Once they have an overall plan for the placement of their features, they can begin planning how they will represent buildings, roads, trees, water, mountains, and other three-dimensional features on the cardboard map.

Week 3   Construct  group   60 minutes

Materials: various art materials, paint, markers, peel and stick labels

Designate a work area for each group. Assemble available craft materials in a central location. Encourage groups to delegate jobs to each person so everyone has something to do.

Once the map is assembled, the children can paint on extra details. Then, once paint and glue have dried, ask groups to mark the cardinal directions and label each land feature on the map. Have them write the feature's name on the label, cut to size, and stick the label on or next to the feature.

Week 4   Present  group   30 minutes

Materials: counter or tabletop space for display, camera (optional)

Determine a place for displaying the 3-D maps, such as the library or multipurpose room. Children can also set up a display in the classroom for a Parent Night, or they can invite other classrooms to view their maps. Ask groups to be prepared to answer questions about their maps. Encourage visitors to ask questions about the absolute and relative locations of features for group members to answer.

Tips for Combination Classrooms

1-2 **For Grade 1 students:** Have children draw a simple flat map of their model that uses symbols to represent features on the map and show their location.

2-3 **For Grade 3 students:** Ask children to write a paragraph that tells how the resources of their map area might be used by the people who live there.

UNIT 2 Short-Term Projects

Use these projects to help children explore geography and maps.

Continental Capitals

 partners   30 minutes

Materials: outline map of North America, reference materials, crayons or colored pencils

Provide partners with untitled maps of North America that include the countries of Central America. Have them do the following:

- Write the name of the continent as the title of the map.

- Label the United States, Canada, Mexico, Guatemala, Belize, El Salvador, Nicaragua, Costa Rica, Honduras, and Panama.

- Color each country a different color.

Playground Map

 group   30 minutes

Materials: paper, pencils, crayons or markers

In advance, copy a four-column, three-row grid onto paper, with the columns labeled A–D and the rows labeled 1–3. Give small groups a copy of the grid. Invite them to design the ideal playground. Remind them that they need to leave room for walkways and play space and that the equipment needs to be safe for all children. Have each group make a list of questions that ask others to find objects or locations. For example: *What is at B-2? (a swing) What is the location of the water fountain? (A-3)* Display the maps and questions, and invite children to find the answers.

36   Social Studies in Action: Resources for the Classroom, Grade 2

Land Brochures

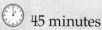 individual   45 minutes

Materials: community or city maps, local newspapers or brochures, drawing paper, crayons or markers

Have children use maps, brochures, and newspapers to research the landforms and points of interest in their city or surrounding community. Demonstrate how to fold drawing paper to make a brochure. Have children create a brochure that advertises their community's landforms and points of interest. Invite children to mark the locations they chose on a map of the community displayed on a bulletin board.

Bat Caves

Bat Caves

Make a Mural

group   30 minutes

Materials: butcher paper, crayons or markers

Ask children to identify the current season and describe its characteristics where they live. Then divide a strip of butcher paper into four sections labeled *Summer, Fall, Winter,* and *Spring.* Divide the class into four groups, and assign each group a season. Have children look out the window and draw the area they see as it might look in their assigned season. Have them write a few sentences describing the characteristics of their assigned season.

UNIT 2 Writing Projects

Children use maps and directions to find their way around every day. Use these prompts to get children writing about maps and directions.

Local Climate

 individual 30 minutes

Ask children to write an essay about the climate in your area. Have children describe the kind of weather in your area, including whether it is hot or cold and the amount of rain. Explain that they should write these essays to introduce your local climate to a new visitor to the area.

Compare and Contrast Landforms

 partners 30 minutes

Have children work in pairs to compare and contrast two landforms. Suggest they record the likenesses and differences on a Venn diagram. Invite children to write paragraphs that describe each landform and then tell how they are alike.

Map Key Riddles

 partners 30 minutes

Provide children with a map that features various map symbols. Invite partners to write riddles on index cards for four different symbols. Ask them to write the riddle on the front of the card and the answer on the back. For example:

Lines are my three sides. I point up and never point down. I rise above the others. What am I? (mountain symbol)

Display the map and the riddles on a bulletin board. Invite the class to read and solve the riddles.

Absolute and Relative Directions

individual **30 minutes**

Ask children to write a letter inviting a friend to their home for a party. Have them each include two sets of directions to the party: one using the absolute location and the other using the relative location of the home. Remind them to include details such as the mailing address and specific landmarks.

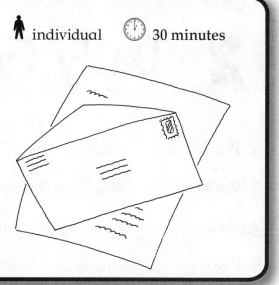

State Brochures

individual **60 minutes**

Locate a large map and research materials about a state other than your own. Help the children to use the map to brainstorm a list of landforms and bodies of water found in the state.

Then, read about some of the geographic features in the state. Pass out construction paper folded into three sections. Ask the children to write a description, list interesting facts, and draw pictures of the geographic features to create a brochure about the state.

Daily Geography

1. **Place**   What is a map?

2. **Place**   What does the title on a map tell you?

3. **Place**   What do you call the pictures on a map that stand for real things?

4. **Place**   What is the list of symbols on a map called?

5. **Location**   Which part of a map helps you find out how far one place is from another?

6. **Location**   What are the lines that form columns and rows and help you find locations on a map called?

7. **Place**   Which city is the state capital of Arizona?

8. **Place**   Which city is the state capital of Wyoming?

9. **Place**   Which city is the capital of the United States of America?

10. **Location**   Between which two states can you find Washington, D.C.?

11. **Place**   What do you call dry land that gets little rain?

12. **Place**   What is the name of a kind of land with a special shape?

13. **Regions**   What is the line around a state or country called?

14. **Location**   Which five states west of the Great Lakes share a boundary with Canada?

15. **Place**   What is a globe?

16. **Place**   What are the largest areas of land on Earth called?

17. **Place**   What are the largest areas of water on Earth called?

18. **Location**   What are four states that touch the Pacific Ocean?

19. **Location**   What are four states that touch the Atlantic Ocean?

20. **Movement**   In which direction would you travel going from the North Pole to the South Pole?

21. **Place**   What is the highest kind of land?

22. **Place**   What kind of land is high, but not as high as a mountain?

23. **Place**   Which kind of land is mostly flat?

24. **Place**   Which is the longest river in the United States?

25. **Location**   Which large bodies of water are between the United States and Canada?

26. **Location**   What is the name of the imaginary line that divides Earth in half?

27. **Location**   On which continent is the South Pole?

28. **Movement**   In which direction would you travel going from Asia to North America?

29. **Location**   Which body of water touches California to the west?

30. **Location**   Which country touches Montana to the north?

Why Character Counts

Patriotism

The feeling of pride people have for their country is called patriotism.

Americans show their patriotism for their country by what they say or do. We show our patriotism when we honor the symbols of the United States. We show patriotism when we display the flag and say the Pledge of Allegiance. We also show patriotism when we sing the national anthem or celebrate national holidays.

- Trustworthiness
- Respect
- Responsibility
- Fairness
- Caring
✓ Patriotism

In Your Own Words:

How do Americans show their patriotism?

Name _____

Character Activity

Look at a map of your state. Find land that is set aside as a national or state park. Find symbols in the map key that show the places of monuments. Use the questions below. Write your answers on the blank lines.

1. What national parks or monuments are found in your state?

_____

_____

_____

_____

2. How does each of these locations honor our country? What would you expect to see at each place?

_____

_____

_____

_____

Economic Literacy

Making Money

Some jobs make goods that other people buy. Goods are things that can be bought and sold. Other jobs provide services that people need. A service is work done by others for pay.

Abrim's parents have jobs. His mother is a doctor. His father works in a bakery. Do they earn money by providing a good or a service?

Abrim's mother helps people get well. She provides a service to other people.

Abrim's father gets up early to bake breads, cookies, and cakes. People buy these goods from him.

What jobs do people in your family have? Do they earn money by providing a good or a service?

Name _____

 **Try It**

Do these problems.

1. Mr. and Mrs. Owens have jobs. Mr. Owens is a plumber.
   Mrs. Owens works in a bookstore. Do Mr. and Mrs. Owens
   provide goods or services? What goods or services does each
   person provide?

   _____

   _____

   _____

2. Think about your community. Write three jobs at which people
   earn money making goods. Write three jobs at which people
   earn money providing a service.

Jobs That Make Goods	Jobs That Provide Services
_____	_____
_____	_____
_____	_____

> **Read About It** The Bill of Rights is a part of our nation's Constitution. The Bill of Rights names the basic rights of each citizen. One of these is the right to own property. This is part of our right to happiness.

1. What does the Bill of Rights say about a citizen's right to own property?

_____

_____

_____

2. Why might someone want to own property?

_____

_____

_____

> **Talk About It** Why does the Bill of Rights protect property?

Name _____

> **Write About It**   The right to own private property is not just about the land. It is our right to own other things like cars, clothes, and books. What property does your family own? How do these things make you and your family happy? Include at least three examples in your answer.

_____

_____

_____

_____

_____

_____

_____

_____

_____

_____

Community Calendar
Unit 3

Materials needed:

*File folder

*Blank calendar

*Tape

*Scissors

*Stapler

*Pencils, plain and colored

*Photograph of friends

Social Studies Skills:

*Working Together

*Charts and Graphs

*Organizing Dates

Reading Skills:

*Sequence

*Point of View

*Summarize

Instructions:

1. Trace and cut out an oval on the top half of the front of the folder. Be sure that the photo you will use will fit behind the oval.

2. Open the folder and tape the photo behind the opening, using the oval as the frame.

Illustrations:

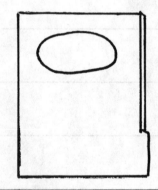

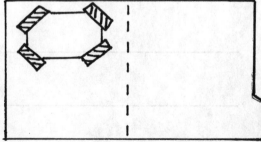

3. Around the oval frame, draw natural resources and ways that people in your community protect them.

4. Staple a blank calendar to the bottom half of the front of the folder. Add the month, days of the week, dates, and year with colored pencils.

5. Add important events that are happening in your school and community. Include recycling days or other dates important to the conservation of natural resources.

The Root Cellar

A readers theatre play about using the land's resources, today and long ago

Cast of Characters

- Narrator
- Grandma
- Aunt Lorraine
- Aunt Arlene
- Dennis, 12-year-old boy

- Susan, 11-year-old girl
- Clark, 7-year-old boy
- Paula, 9-year-old girl
- Teri, 11-year-old girl
- David, 9-year-old boy

Narrator: Several children are playing a game of hide-and-seek in the fruit orchard of a family farm. Dennis is leaning against an apple tree, his eyes hidden as he counts to 50.

Teri: (softly) Come with me, Paula. I have the perfect hiding place.

Narrator: Teri takes Paula to a door. She opens the door and they walk down a flight of stairs together. They enter a very tiny room lined with shelves. It is sort of like a basement. The only difference is that it has dirt walls and floors.

Paula: What is this place?

Teri: It's Grandma's root cellar.

Clark: I don't see any roots.

Narrator: Both girls whirl around to face Clark, Paula's younger brother.

Paula: Did you follow us?

Teri: It's okay. Clark asked a good question. This place is only called a root cellar. It stays nice and cool in the summer and not too cold in the winter because it is partly underground.

Paula: Grandma must store her food in this cellar. I see fruits and vegetables in glass jars on the shelves.

Clark: Is a root cellar like a refrigerator?

Teri: Yes. Before there were refrigerators, people used root cellars to keep food fresh for the winter. The root cellar is for storing things like potatoes, pumpkins, and squash. See the basket of potatoes?

Narrator: Two other children appear at the door.

Dennis: There you are! I found you. You know, when you hide, it is best to be quiet. I could hear you all the way across the yard.

David: What is going on? Is this where you hid?

Paula: We hid here. Clark followed us in.

Clark: We were just looking at Grandma's big root cellar.

Dennis: Where is that?

Paula: He is talking about this place. It is called the root cellar. It is where Grandma keeps things during the winter. It is like a big refrigerator.

Grandma: Hello? What are you kids doing down here?

David: We were playing hide-and-seek. Teri, Paula, and Clark hid in here.

Grandma: Well, it looks more like a party.

Clark: Grandma, why don't you buy a refrigerator?

Teri: (laughing) He thinks this is the only refrigerator you have.

Grandma: Oh. Of course, I have a refrigerator. The root cellar is better for storing things we use later. Otherwise, the refrigerator would be too full.

Narrator: Everyone walks up the stairs into the daylight outside. Aunt Arlene and Aunt Lorraine join them.

Dennis: Grandma, people did things differently when you were little, didn't they?

Grandma: Oh my, yes. Your grandfather used a horse and plow to turn over the soil.

Aunt Arlene: I remember when he bought the tractor.

Aunt Lorraine: We also had to help spread cow manure over the garden. I bet that is a job you would like to help with.

David: No, thank you. Why did you do that?

Aunt Arlene: It was part of our chores. It made the soil better.

Narrator: Susan runs toward the family.

Susan: Isn't anyone going to find me?

Dennis: I forgot about you! Where were you hiding?

Susan: I was in the chicken coop. I think the chickens were getting pretty mad.

Teri: Good thing you gave up. You could have been in there until dinnertime. Here, you have a feather in your hair.

Paula: Grandma, can we see if there are any eggs?

Grandma: I just gathered them this morning, but you can see if there are any new ones.

Teri: Let's go!

The End

Simulations and Games

Transportation Alphabet

Review with children different kinds of transportation, both present and past. Then divide the class into small groups. Have children begin with the letter *A* and take turns naming a form of transportation for each letter in the alphabet, such as *airplane* for *A*, *bus* for *B*, and *car* for *C*. When a child gets stuck on a letter, he or she is out. Play should continue until just one child remains in the game. You may want to have a finals match with the winners from each small group playing again, this time with the rest of the class as an audience. **GAME**

Farming Past and Present
Write various farming tasks on notecards, such as *plant seeds*, *water crops*, *plow soil*, *harvest crops*, and *take products to market*. Have children work in pairs. Place cards face down in a stack. One child pretends to be a farmer from the past and the other a farmer from the present. Pairs select one card and read the task, and each partner describes how the task was done in their time period. For example, a farmer of the past might say: *I plow the soil with a horse and a plow*, while the present farmer might say: *I plow my field with a tractor and a cultivator*. **SIMULATION**

We Use Resources
Write each of the following words three times on separate cards: *Air*, *Land*, *Trees*, and *Water*. Have small groups play a game in which they take turns selecting a card, naming the resource, and describing how they use the resource. **GAME**

Recycling Inventions Gather together various objects set to become trash such as milk cartons, gallon jugs, paper towel tubes, plastic utensils, and packaging materials. Be sure all objects are clean. Invite children to select an object. Ask them to imagine they are scientists and their job is to recycle the object by using it a new way. Invite children to explain the new use of the object to the group. **SIMULATION**

World Travelers Divide children into groups and provide each group with a globe. Ask children to imagine they will travel from a place in the world to the community where they live. Invite children to take turns as they cover their eyes, spin the globe, and touch their finger to one spot to stop it. Have the child trace a route from this spot to home. Then, have the group discuss how they would travel from the place to their home.

Ask children to imagine they are traveling today or long ago and recount their travels accordingly. For example, to travel today from Cape Town, South Africa, to Chicago, Illinois, they might take a boat, then a train, then a car. Long ago, they might have taken a boat, then a wagon, and walked to their final destination. **GAME**

3 Long-Term Project

FARMING BULLETIN BOARD

Use this project to help children think more in depth about how farmers use resources, in the past and in the present.

Week 1 Introduce group  30 minutes

Materials: paper, pencils

Introduce the project by making a chart that names some of the similarities and differences between farming long ago and farming today. Help children name similarities and differences related to machinery and technology; uses of resources such as air, water, land, trees, and fuel; types and numbers of crops and/or animals; seed planting, crop growth, harvest, and transportation to market; pests and problems; and people who worked on the farm.

Divide the class into two groups. Explain that each group will design and create a bulletin board display. One group will show farming in the past. The other group will show farming today. You may want to suggest the following ideas:

• *To show farming in the past:* A farmer plows his field with an ox and a plow. His children plant seeds by hand. His wife carries water in buckets from a nearby pond. There are stumps of trees that have been chopped down to make room for crops. This family grows a variety of crops and raises many animals.

• *To show farming today:* A farmer rides a combine tractor in a large field. Workers in the foreground pick corn that is ready for harvest. A transport truck is parked near a large modern barn and silo. A windmill turns in the background. Trees form a windbreak around the farm. There is evidence only of a single crop being grown and harvested: corn.

Week 2   Plan

 group 30 minutes

Materials: research materials, drawing paper, pencils, markers or crayons, scissors, butcher paper

Encourage groups to look at pictures for ideas on what their half of the board will show. Suggest they make a list of possible pictures, and have each group member select one to draw. Explain that they will arrange drawings on butcher paper the same size as their bulletin board space. Point out that some group members need to draw a background on the butcher paper that shows sky, the farm in the distance, and the farm up close. Ask them to complete and cut out all drawings.

Week 3   Construct

 group 60 minutes

Materials: art supplies, glue, bulletin board space, stapler

After each group has finished their drawings and background, have them work together to glue all pictures into place. While the glue is drying, ask groups to make labels and captions to explain the various details they have shown in their farm scene. Staple the completed scenes to each half of the bulletin board.

Week 4   Present

 group 30 minutes

Have each group present what their half of the board shows, and answer questions from the rest of the class. Invite other classrooms and children's parents or guardians to view the bulletin board as well.

Tips for Combination Classrooms

1-2 **For Grade 1 students:** Help children illustrate how, on average, the size of farming families decreased during the last century.

2-3 **For Grade 3 students:** Have children include local geographical features particular to the nearest farming area.

UNIT 3 Short-Term Projects

Use these projects to help children explore the land and its resources.

Geography Poster

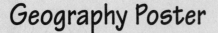 partners 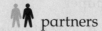 30 minutes

Materials: old magazines, newspapers, scissors, construction paper, glue, crayons or markers

Have partners cut out pictures of various landforms and bodies of water. Ask them to determine how they will sort their pictures into two groups, such as rural and urban geography or land and water geography. Invite partners to make a two-column chart, title the chart, and title each column. Have them glue the pictures into the correct columns.

Charting Map Symbols

 partners 30 minutes

Materials: various maps, paper, pencil

Display a variety of maps. Have partners observe and compare the symbols used to show landforms, roads, and human-made points of interest. Invite partners to make a chart that shows the different ways maps show each category

Airport

School

of features. For example, children may draw the different kinds of symbols for roads or draw the various icons that represent public buildings such as schools, hospitals, and airports. Encourage children to label each symbol they include on their chart.

Favorite Farm Produce

 class  30 minutes

Materials: paper, pencil, crayons or markers

Ask children to complete a survey and make a farm produce picture graph of their findings. Help survey the children to find their favorite vegetables. Then encourage children to make a picture graph that shows the top four or five choices. Remind them to use a picture to show the number of votes for each choice.

Our Favorite Vegetables	
Carrots	🥕🥕🥕🥕🥕
Lettuce	🥬🥬🥬🥬
Tomatoes	🍅🍅🍅🍅🍅
Peppers	🍎🍎🍎

Air, Water, and Land

 partners 45 minutes

Materials: construction paper, crayons or markers

Remind children that air, water, and land are natural resources we use. Invite children to work in pairs to create a poster that shows some of these uses. Have pairs divide a sheet of construction paper into three sections and label each *Air, Water,* and *Land.* Suggest children brainstorm uses for each resource and then draw an illustration for four uses that will be placed in the appropriate column. Encourage children to include a phrase or caption. For example, wind chimes might be shown with the caption: *Air is used to make music.*

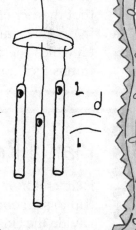

UNIT 3 Writing Projects

Use these prompts to help children explore how people use natural resources and how we conserve and recycle our resources.

A Journey

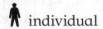 individual 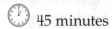 45 minutes

Provide children with maps of their state. Starting at the northern border, ask them to trace a journey across the state that ends at the southern border. Suggest children write journal entries that tell the distance they travel each day, the cities they pass through, the directions they go, and the landforms and points of interest they see. Invite children to share their journals as the class follows along on a state map.

Dear Friend

 individual  30 minutes

Show children photographs of homes in different types of environments, such as a house in the suburbs, a high-rise apartment building in the city, a hut in the country, and a houseboat on the water. Then ask children to imagine that they live in one of the homes. Have each child write a letter to a friend in another part of the world. The letter should describe the land or water on which the child lives, the kinds of work that family members do, and the things that adults and children do for fun.

Plan a Resource Field Trip

 group 30 minutes

Help children imagine they are planning a field trip to see some of their state's natural resources. Divide the class into groups and help children brainstorm places where they can see natural resources in use. Some examples might be a wind farm, a hydroelectric dam, a community pond, a paper mill, or a farm. Ask groups to plan the field trip, telling the order in which they will visit each place, how long they will stay, and what others should expect to see.

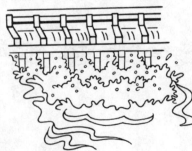

Recycle and Conserve

 individual 30 minutes

Tell children that they will make posters that remind others to recycle or conserve resources. As a class, help children brainstorm how students can help conserve and recycle supplies around their school. Possibilities include: recycling glass, aluminum, and plastic in the lunch room, using scraps of paper for art projects, and reusing the back sides of writing paper. List their ideas on the board. Ask children to choose a topic and create a poster. Remind them to use big letters that are easy to read and interesting, eye-catching colors. Post completed posters near locations where they can serve as reminders.

Letter to the Editor

 group 30 minutes

Remind children that pollution is anything that makes the air, water, or land dirty. Discuss with children an area of their community that needs to be cleaned up. Explain that citizens often write letters to the editor of a newspaper stating a problem and how they think it can be solved. Invite children to work in groups to write their own letters to the editor. Encourage children to write about an area that needs to be cleaned up and include how they think it can be done. Post the letters for other children to read.

Conservation Brochure

 individual 30 minutes

Explain that a brochure is a folded piece of paper that has words and pictures to give people information. Invite children to create a brochure that tells others how to recycle and conserve our resources. Suggest they make an eye-catching cover with a title. Have children include several drawings, each with directions that tell how to conserve or recycle a particular resource. Display completed brochures on a bulletin board for others to read.

UNIT 3 Daily Geography

1. Place   Which city is the state capital of Minnesota?

2. Place   Which city is the state capital of Iowa?

3. Movement   In which direction would you travel if you went from New York to California?

4. Movement   Which state must you travel through to go straight from Montana to Washington?

5. Movement   Which states would you pass through going in a straight line west from Kansas to California?

6. Location   Which of these states share a border?
Wyoming and New Mexico
Texas and New Mexico
Kansas and New Mexico

7. Place   Which states touch Maryland to the west?

8. Location   If you were in Boise, in which state's capital would you be?

9. Place   Which city is the state capital of Ohio?

10. Location   Is the capital city of Austin located in Texas or Montana?

11. Regions   What do you call a large community that is made up of many neighborhoods?

12. Regions   What do you call an area in the country where people and buildings are far apart?

13. Location   Is Chicago, Illinois, an urban or rural area?

14. Regions   What is a community near a large city called?

15. Place Which city is the capital of Massachusetts and the state's largest city?

16. Location Which of the following state capitals is closest to Bismarck, North Dakota?
Denver
Atlanta
Philadelphia

17. Place Which state capital is named for an ocean?

18. Place Which state capitals are named after a President of the United States?

19. Place Which state capitals have the state names in their own names?

20. Movement Imagine that the governor of Colorado will travel to the capital of Missouri. In which direction will he or she travel?

21. Human-Environment Interactions In which state capital would you be in the desert?
Phoenix, Arizona
Richmond, Virginia
Helena, Montana

22. Human-Environment Interactions In which of these state capitals would you be near mountains?
Denver, Colorado
Topeka, Kansas
Lincoln, Nebraska

23. Place Which is the largest of the seven continents?

24. Place Which is the smallest of the seven continents?

25. Location Which continent is directly south of North America?

26. Movement Imagine that the leader from Canada's capital will travel to our nation's capital. In which direction will he or she travel?

27. Location Which four states touch Mexico?

28. Location Which state touches Canada, the Atlantic Ocean, and only one other state?

29. Regions Which of these countries is a part of South America?
Bolivia
Canada
Jordan

30. Place Is Beijing or Tokyo the capital city of China?

Why Character Counts

Caring

People show they care when they work to make things better for other people.

You can show you care at home. You might do extra chores at home when a family member is not feeling well. You might help a new student feel welcomed. You might cheer up a sad friend. Helping others shows that you care.

People can show care in the community. People can collect food, clothing, and money to help others in need. They can care for those who lost their homes in a fire.

In Your Own Words:

What does it mean to be caring?

_____

_____

_____

Name _____

Character Activity

Interview a classmate to find out how he or she shows caring.
Use the questions below. Write your answers on the blank lines.

1. How do other people show they care about you?

_____

_____

2. What can you do to show you care for the community?

_____

_____

3. How can you show others that you care?

_____

_____

_____

_____

UNIT 3 Economic Literacy

Make a Budget

A budget is a plan for spending and saving money. Families make budgets to spend their money. They buy things to keep them safe and healthy. They want to buy other things that are fun. They save money to buy things in the future.

Each week, Amy earns $10.00 as her allowance. Amy uses a budget to help her make choices about the things she buys. She pays for her own school supplies. She also wants to buy fun things like books or toys. She saves some of the money. How can Amy budget her money?

This is the budget Amy made for each week's allowance:

$3.00 is for school supplies and activities.

$3.00 is for spending money.

$4.00 is for saving.

Do you think Amy has made a good budget? Why or why not? Explain why it is important to make saving money a part of a budget.

Name _____

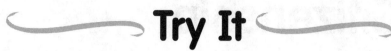
Do these problems.

1. Amy would like to buy a new bicycle. A bicycle costs a lot of money. Amy's allowance for one week is not enough to pay for a bicycle. What can Amy do so she will be able to buy a bicycle?

_____

_____

2. Juan earns $5.00 each week. He will spend $1.00 to pay for supplies he uses at school. He wants to use some of the money to do fun things with his friends. He wants to buy a new baseball mitt, but it costs $20.00. Make a budget to help Juan spend and save for the things he wants to buy.

_____

_____

_____

_____

_____

UNIT 3 Citizenship

> **Read About It** The government works to make fair laws. The Constitution and Declaration of Independence list some of these fair laws. These laws give all citizens the same rights. Where you come from, your skin color, your religion, or whether you are a boy or a girl does not change your rights.

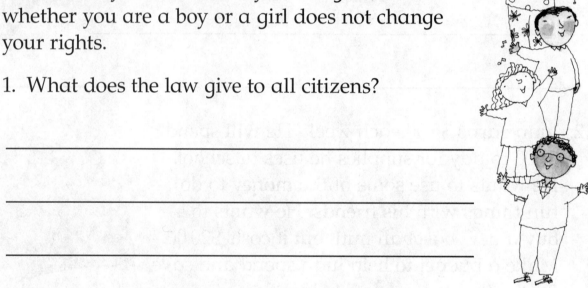

1. What does the law give to all citizens?

   _____

   _____

   _____

2. What does not change your rights?

   _____

   _____

   _____

> **Talk About It** The Declaration of Independence states that "all men are created equal." What does this mean? How has this idea spread to women and other people?

Name _____

How can your rights help you become a hero in your community? Write a paragraph about this. Include acts or ideas that will help make you a hero in your community.

_____

_____

_____

_____

_____

_____

_____

_____

_____

_____

_____

Heroes Across Time...Line
Unit 4

Materials needed:

*Drawing Paper

*Tape or glue

*Crayons, colored pencils, or markers

*Scissors

Social Studies Skills:

*Time Line

*The Past

*Sequencing Events

Reading Skills:

*Sequence

*Cause and Effect

*Summarize

Instructions:

1. Decide on a hero from the past or the present to write about. Copy the illustration to make a time line page for each year you write about in the life of a hero.

2. In each section, write about an important event in the person's life and add a picture or a photograph.

Illustrations:

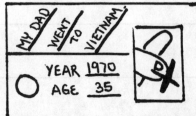

3. Glue all the sections together in order.

4. Share the time line and illustrations that show the sequence of events in the life of your hero.

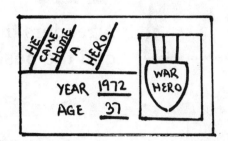

HE CAME HOME A HERO.

YEAR 1972
AGE 37

WAR HERO

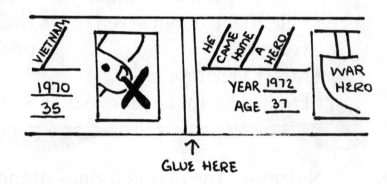

VIETNAM
1970
35

HE CAME HOME A HERO.

YEAR 1972
AGE 37

WAR HERO

↑
GLUE HERE

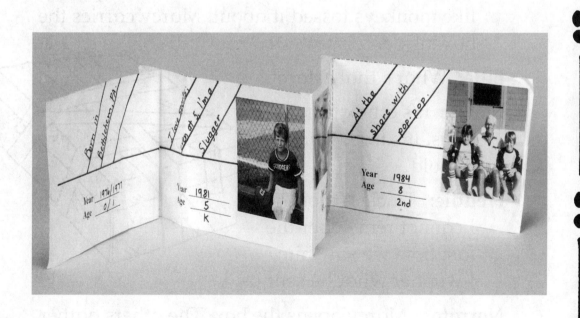

The Old Jacket

A readers theatre play about families and the past

Cast of Characters

- Narrator
- Marcy Klein, a teenager
- Ellie Klein, about seven years old
- Mrs. Klein, mother
- Freddie Klein, 11 years old
- Max Percy, Freddie's friend
- Uncle Arnold, great-uncle of Mrs. Klein, 88 years old
- Sound Effects

Narrator: The doorbell rings at the Klein home.

Sound Effects: Ding-dong!

Narrator: Marcy opens the door. A delivery person hands her a large box. The box is beat up. It looks like monkeys tossed it about. Marcy carries the box inside.

Ellie: What's that, Marcy?

Marcy: It's a box for all of us. It's from Uncle Arnold.

Freddie: Uncle Arnold? I cannot remember the last time we saw him. I wonder what he sent us.

Narrator: Marcy opens the box. The others gather around her.

Marcy: It's a jacket. It's old, brown, and beat up. It looks like a soldier's jacket.

Freddie: Let me try it on!

Narrator: Freddie tries on the jacket. He feels the lumpy sleeves. He puts his hands in the pockets. His fingers come out the bottoms.

Ellie: It's torn. The lining is coming out, too.

Freddie: It feels rough and stiff. And it has cracks all over it.

Max: (sniffing) It smells funny, like an old briefcase.

Mrs. Klein: It's made of leather, Max. This must be the jacket Uncle Arnold wore when he flew airplanes. That was many, many years ago, during World War II.

Freddie: Uncle Arnold was young enough to fly a plane?

Mrs. Klein: He was young at one time. He was very handsome, too. His hair was dark brown. It was not white, like it is now.

Marcy: I never knew Uncle Arnold was a pilot. He never talked about it. I don't remember hearing his war stories.

Mrs. Klein: Some people who fought in wars don't like to talk about it. It brings back sad memories.

Ellie: Does Uncle Arnold walk slowly because of the war?

Mrs. Klein: He walks slowly because he is 88 years old. But when he was young, he could run fast.

Freddie: Why did Uncle Arnold send us this old jacket?

Mrs. Klein: He wants to keep the past and our family history alive. I think his jacket makes a wonderful gift.

Max: We have my grandmother's piano in our house.

Mrs. Klein: Yes, Max, it's nice when families hand things down.

Marcy: We keep Grandpa Ben's shaving mug in the cabinet. (pause) Why don't we call Uncle Arnold?

Mrs. Klein: That's a great idea! Let's do it.

Freddie: Can I talk to him first?

Narrator: Mrs. Klein enters Uncle Arnold's phone number on the speaker phone. Everyone can talk and hear. There is quiet in the room.

Sound Effects: R-r-r-r-ring! R-r-r-r-ring! (telephone ringing)

Uncle Arnold: (coughs, then speaks softly) Hello?

Freddie: Uncle Arnold? It's me, Freddie.

Uncle Arnold: (softly) Freddie?

Freddie: Yes, Freddie Klein. We are all here except for Dad.

All the Kleins: (together, loudly) Hi, Uncle Arnold!

Ellie: (excitedly, when it is quiet) And it's me, Ellie! We got the jacket.

All the Kleins: (loudly again) Thanks for the jacket.

Narrator: There is quiet on the line. Everybody waits for Uncle Arnold to say something.

Mrs. Klein: Unc, are you there?

Uncle Arnold: (after a few seconds) Yes, I'm right here.

Narrator: Ellie, Freddie, Max, Marcy, and Mrs. Klein listen hard. They can almost hear a smile over the phone.

Uncle Arnold: I can't zip up that old jacket anymore. My belly got too big. (coughs) I've got a new one now that fits better.

Mrs. Klein: Oh, Unc. We miss you. We're so glad for this special gift.

Narrator: Uncle Arnold coughs again. Then he does what he has never done before. He begins to tell his family about the war. He speaks softly and slowly. Everyone listens hard.

Uncle Arnold: Let me tell you about the first time I flew a plane by myself. I had bad luck and good luck. Which shall I tell you about first?

The End

Simulations and Games

Pick-a-Word Relay Have two relay teams line up to play while the rest of the class watches. In front of each team, display the same four vocabulary word cards on the chalk ledge. Give a cloze sentence as a clue for one of the words, and have the first member of each team go to the chalk ledge and pick the correct word. Replace those two cards with new ones, and repeat until all team members have had a turn. The team with the most correct choices wins. **GAME**

Grid-Tac-Toe To play this game, you will need postcards showing national landmarks, a numbered/lettered 3 x 3 grid (with squares slightly larger than the postcards), index cards naming squares on the grid by letter and number, and checkers. Invite pairs of children to play Grid-Tac-Toe. Have children place the postcards on the grid and take turns drawing from the stack of cards. Players must name the building or monument that is in the square indicated on the card. If the answer is correct, the player takes the postcard and places one of his or her checkers on the square. If not, the postcard is left in place and the index card is returned to the bottom of the pile. The first player to have three checkers in a row wins. **GAME**

Signing the Declaration of Independence To do this simulation, you will need a large sheet of paper or posterboard to represent the Declaration of Independence. Begin by reminding children that 56 leaders representing the 13 colonies signed the Declaration of Independence. Then tell children that they are going to act out the signing of this important document. Have children imagine that they are the signers of the Declaration of Independence. Have each child in turn come up to the front of the classroom. Before the child signs the document, have him or her make a statement about its importance. **SIMULATION**

The Native American Hand Game   Begin this game with a brief class discussion about Native American games. Explain that many of the games helped Native American children develop the skills they would need as adults, as well as provided fun. Tell children that they are going to play the Hand Game, a popular guessing game in many tribes. Organize them into two teams.

To prepare for this game, you will need two identical objects, such as buttons or small stones, and ten counting sticks, such as toothpicks or chenille sticks. Mark a dot on one of the objects. Set out the counting sticks, and give one team the objects.

To play the game, one member of the team with the objects conceals an object in each hand. A member of the opposing team then points to the hand he or she thinks contains the marked object. If the choice is correct, the guessing team wins a counting stick; if not, it loses a stick. When all the members of each team have had a turn, the teams switch roles. When one team wins all the counting sticks, the game is over. **GAME**

Revolutionary War Time Line Challenge   Create several sets of sentence strips that contain the events leading up to the Revolutionary War. Mix up the strips so they are in a random order. Divide the class into small groups. Instruct each group to place the events in the proper chronological order. The team that completes the task correctly in the shortest amount of time is the winner. **GAME**

UNIT 4 Long-Term Project

A BIOGRAPHY QUILT

Use this project to help children think in depth about the life of a hero.

Week 1 Introduce

 group 30 minutes

Materials: paper, pencils, resource materials

Introduce the project by discussing a hero from the past that children know well. Ask questions such as, "What has this person done that has made life better for others?" Discuss some of the events from the person's life. Explain to children that they will work in groups to make a biography quilt for a hero. Each square of the quilt will tell about an important event in the life of the hero they choose.

Divide the class into groups. Encourage groups to choose a hero and help them begin to collect information about this individual. Help children use resource materials to find events in the person's life. Ask them to make a list of six events they think are important to share with others. You may want to suggest children look for the following: childhood events connected to why the person became a hero; any discoveries, inventions, or places the hero is known for; prizes or awards the hero won or monuments that were built to honor the hero.

Week 2 Plan

 group 30 minutes

Materials: construction paper, pencils, crayons or markers

Explain that each group's quilt will be made from paper and have a total of six squares. Have children plan and list the six events their quilt will show. Then encourage children to work together to draw a picture for each event. Ask them to write a caption for each square.

Week 3 Construct

 group 30 minutes

Materials: butcher paper, glue, markers or crayons

Assist children as they construct their quilt. Demonstrate how to space the squares to form a 2-by-3 square grid on butcher paper. Suggest that children check the order of the squares before they glue them into place. Once the glue has dried, show children how to use a marker or crayon to make hatch marks or crossed lines along the edge of each square. Explain that these form the "stitching lines" on a quilt. Have groups write the name, birth date, and date of death at the top in the border of the quilt. Suggest each group member sign the quilt on the bottom border.

Harriet Tubman

Week 4 Present

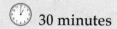 group 30 minutes

Materials: hanging space for display, camera (optional)

Find a place to display the quilts. If possible, take a picture of each quilt surrounded by the children who made it.

Tips for Combination Classrooms

1–2 **For Grade 1 students:** Have children choose for their quilt one of the people connected to the Declaration of Independence.

2–3 **For Grade 3 students:** Ask children to focus on the life of an equal rights hero such as Dolores Huerta, Rosa Parks, or Cesar Chavez.

UNIT 4 Short-Term Projects

Use these projects to help children explore change and history.

Long Ago and Yesterday

 group 45 minutes

Materials: resource materials, construction paper, crayons, markers

Remind the class that both "long ago" and "yesterday" mean time that has passed. "Yesterday" means the time that has just passed, while "long ago" usually means months or years ago. Divide the class into groups. Ask each group to decide how they can use picture pairs to show yesterday and long ago. Have each member of the group draw pictures that show yesterday or long ago. On the back, label the picture. Use the pictures like flash cards. Ask children to decide if the picture shows yesterday or long ago. They may use the labels on the back to check their answers.

Washington, D.C. Landmarks

 individual 30 minutes

Materials: pictures of Washington, D.C. landmarks, drawing paper, crayons

Show the children pictures of important national landmarks located on or near the National Mall in Washington, D.C. Landmarks could include the Capitol Building, the Washington Monument, the Supreme Court, Arlington National Cemetery, the White House, the Library of Congress, the Lincoln Memorial, the Jefferson Memorial, or the Vietnam Veterans Memorial. Ask the students to draw a picture of one of these landmarks. Make sure they accurately label the picture. For advanced students, ask them to write a sentence describing the landmark.

Hero Mystery Box

 group 30 minutes

Materials: shoeboxes, art supplies, crayons or markers

Have children work in groups to make a hero mystery box. Explain to children that they will put together a collection of items that represent the work and life of a hero. For example, a mystery box for Benjamin Franklin might include eyeglasses made of pipe cleaners, a small paper kite, a rolled-up cylinder of paper tied with a ribbon and titled "The Declaration of Independence," and a construction paper booklet titled "Poor Richard's Almanack." Ask groups to write their hero's name inside the lid and tape a flap of paper over it. Display the mystery boxes. Have children guess the hero each box represents, checking their guesses against the name under the paper flap inside the lid.

Make a Monument

 group 45 minutes

Materials: resource books and photographs of monuments, paper, pencils, craft supplies

Explain to children that we sometimes build monuments or memorials to honor our heroes. Display pictures of monuments and memorials such as the Washington Monument, Mount Rushmore, or the Vietnam Veterans Memorial. Invite children to name structures in their own community that honor a hero. Have children work in small groups to design a monument for a hero of their choosing. Provide groups with art and craft supplies they can use to construct their monument. Display the completed monuments to share with others.

Writing Projects

Use these prompts to get children writing about history.

Interview Questions

 partners   30 minutes

Have partners think about traveling back in time to the days of the Revolutionary War. Ask them to discuss which of the Revolutionary War heroes they would like to meet. Once they have selected an individual, have them work together to write a list of questions they would ask this person.

Symbols of Our Nation

 individual   45 minutes

Provide children with pictures of sights to see in our nation's capital such as the Washington Monument, the Lincoln Memorial, the Capitol building, and the White House. Invite children to refer to the picture as they write a descriptive paragraph about one of the sights. Then have them add a second paragraph that tells why they think this sight is an important symbol of our nation.

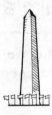

My Hero

 individual   15 minutes

Remind children that heroes are not just famous people or people who lived long ago. People in our lives today can be heroes. Invite children to name someone they know that they think of as a hero. Point out that this person may have done something brave or important, or may have helped them in some way. Invite children to draw a picture of their hero. Ask them to complete this sentence and write it under the picture:

_____ *is my hero because* _____.

A Ship's Log

 individual  30 minutes

Tell children that when the settlers were crossing the ocean to come to the colonies, the ship's captain kept a log, or a journal, to record what happened during the voyage. Invite children to imagine that they are the captain of a ship bringing settlers, and ask them to write a log entry. Suggest that they include some thoughts about the ship, the weather conditions, and their feelings about the journey and their hopes for what life would be like in the new land.

Riddles of the Past

 group  30 minutes

Gather unusual utensils or tools from the past that would be largely unknown to children today, such as a melon baller, ricer, potato masher, or pastry cutter. Divide the class into small groups and give one tool to each group. Invite groups to discuss its features. Then, privately, tell each group the true use of the tool. Invite groups to write a riddle about their tool for their classmates to solve. Display the tools and riddles.

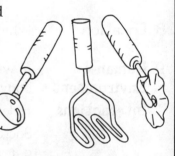

Write a Journal

 group  45 minutes

Ask children to write a journal entry that records as many of the previous day's activities as they can recall. Then have children share their journal entries in small groups. Ask groups to list activities that would be the same between themselves and children long ago. Examples might include going to school, making their beds, eating breakfast, and playing with friends. Then have them list differences, such as riding a bus to school, working on a computer, or using a calculator for math. Invite groups to share their lists.

Daily Geography

1. Place	Which kind of body of water is long and flows across the land?
2. Movement	If you sailed from Florida to Texas, in which direction would you travel?
3. Location	Which state touches both Mexico and the Gulf of Mexico?
4. Location	Which two states touch both Canada and the Pacific Ocean?
5. Location	Which body of water do both Alaska and Hawaii touch?
6. Location	Sometimes part of the border of a state or country is a river. Which river is part of the border between Texas and Oklahoma?
7. Location	Which river is the border between California and Arizona?
8. Location	Which river is the border between Nebraska and Iowa?
9. Human-Environment Interactions	In which of these state capitals would you be nearest a large body of water? Helena, Montana Sacramento, California Salt Lake City, Utah
10. Location	Which body of water touches the states between Texas and Florida?
11. Location	Which state touches large bodies of water on the east, the west, and the south?
12. Place	Which state capital is named for a large, salty lake?
13. Place	In which one of the 50 states would you be if you were in Annapolis?
14. Place	Which capital city is linked to its state's largest city by the Hudson River?
15. Location	St. Paul has what twin city on the other side of the Mississippi River?

16. Place   What are the names of the five Great Lakes?

17. Location   Which of the following capital cities is closest to the largest Great Lake?
St. Paul, Minnesota
Cheyenne, Wyoming
Columbus, Ohio

18. Place   Which two states have four straight lines as borders?

19. Place   Which is the longest river in the world?

20. Place   Which mountain is the highest in the world?

21. Place   What do farmers in dry places use to water their crops?

22. Place   What do you call a map that shows the resources and products of a place?

23. Place   What do you call the kind of weather a place has over time?

24. Place   If you lived in the capital city of Washington, would the climate more likely be dry or wet?

25. Place   If you lived in the capital city of Minnesota, would the climate more likely be cold or hot?

26. Place   If you lived in the capital city of Arizona, would the climate more likely be dry or wet?

27. Human-Environment Interactions   In which of these cities would you be nearest a large river?
Portland, Oregon
Birmingham, Alabama
Reno, Nevada

28. Location   Which of these state capitals is closest to the Mississippi River?
Atlanta
Frankfort
Baton Rouge

29. Location   Which river is the border between Ohio and Kentucky?

30. Movement   If you took a boat down the Mississippi River from St. Paul, Minnesota, in which direction would you travel?

Why Character Counts

Responsibility

- **Trustworthiness**
- **Respect**
- ✓ **Responsibility**
- **Fairness**
- **Caring**
- **Patriotism**

A responsibility is a job that we must do. Citizens in the United States have many responsibilities. We have to follow the laws of our community, state, and country. It is our job to know about these laws so we can obey them. It is also our job to respect the rights of other people.

At home you may have responsibilities. It might be your job to help clear the table or clean up your room.

In Your Own Words:

Some people believe it is the responsibility of citizens to vote. What do you think? Why?

_____

_____

_____

Name _____

Character Activity

Answer the questions below. Write your answers on the blank lines.

1. Being responsible means doing your part. In the classroom, doing your part can be as simple as returning supplies to where they belong. In what ways do you do your part in your classroom?

_____

_____

_____

2. We have a responsibility to help others. What do you do to help others at home?

_____

_____

_____

3. We all have a responsibility to make our community a good place to live. How do you show that you care about your community?

_____

_____

_____

Economic Literacy

UNIT 4

Producers and Consumers

Have you ever seen someone buy something at the store? People who buy goods or services are called consumers. Someone who sells or makes goods or services is called a producer.

Missy Sims runs a pet-care shop. Missy takes care of other people's dogs. She gives the dogs baths. She combs their fur and trims their nails. She even has pretty collars and leashes for sale in her shop.

Missy Sims offers a service. She is a producer. Who are the consumers?

The dog owners are the consumers. They pay for the services.

Name _____

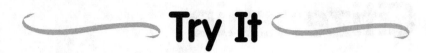

Try It

Do these problems.

1. Mr. Porto owns a toy store. He
   sells stuffed animals, games, toy
   trucks, and purses. If you buy
   a toy for a friend's birthday, he
   will wrap it for you. Is Mr. Porto
   a consumer or producer? Why?

_____

_____

_____

_____

2. Mrs. Garcia owns a flower shop. She sells pretty
   flowers. She delivers the flowers to homes and
   shops. Mrs. Garcia delivered flowers to the pet
   care shop for Missy's birthday. While she was
   there, Mrs. Garcia bought a collar for her dog.
   Is Mrs. Garcia a producer, a consumer, or both?
   Why?

_____

_____

_____

▶ **Read About It**   In the Bill of Rights, the First Amendment names some of our basic freedoms. It protects the freedom of speech. The freedom of speech means Americans can say what they think about something. It allows people to talk about what they think is right and wrong.

1. Name a freedom protected by the First Amendment.

_____

_____

2. What does the First Amendment allow Americans to do?

_____

_____

▶ **Talk About It**   What are examples of times when freedom of speech may be harmful to others?

I think...

Freedom of Speech

Name _____

> **Write About It** Cesar Chavez wanted to help migrant workers. He thought the workers were treated unfairly. He held meetings to tell groups about their rights. Newspapers reported on the poor working conditions to the public. New laws were passed to protect the migrant workers. What First Amendment freedom did Chavez use in his fight to help the workers? How can people use freedom of speech to change things we think are wrong?

_____

_____

_____

_____

_____

_____

_____

_____

_____

Lunch Bag Family Tree
Unit 5

Materials needed:
*Lunch-size paper bag
*Scissors
*Glue or glue stick
*Family photos or drawings

Social Studies Skills:
*Family Heritage
*Celebrations
*Cultures

Reading Skills:
*Cause and Effect
*Summarize
*Compare and Contrast

Illustrations:

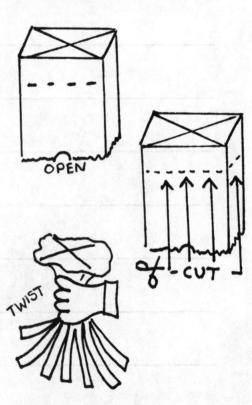

Instructions:

1. Open the lunch-size paper bag.

2. Holding the bag from the open end, cut down all the folded pleats to the first crease line to make strips.

3. Continue cutting strips around the bag approximately the same width.

4. Grab the bag above the flat base and twist the base to form the trunk.

5. Students may enjoy a few "pounds" on the base of the tree to keep it flat.

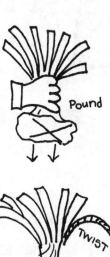

6. Take each strip and twist it fairly tightly to form a branch. Be sure to twist the branch all the way to the end.

7. For variety, you may want to cut the end of some strips to form two small branches.

8. Glue faces of family members on the branches, starting with yourself at the top.

9. Invite students to present their family trees to the class. Other options include writing stories about themselves and/or their families.

Heroes

A readers theatre play about heroes

Cast of Characters

- Reader 1
- Reader 2
- Reader 3
- Reader 4
- Reader 5
- Reader 6

Reader 1: A hero is a person who knows how to think and behave.

Reader 2: A hero is a person who has a good idea and acts brave.

Reader 3: An inventor is a hero who makes something new.

Reader 4: Scientists who cure diseases are heroes, too.

Reader 5: Explorers can be heroes when they find new lands.

Reader 6: Heroes are people who lend a helping hand.

Reader 1: We know many heroes by the way they act.

All: Good ideas and acts make a hero.

Reader 2: And that's a fact!

Reader 3: Eleanor Roosevelt was a President's wife.

Reader 4: She saw people in some countries had a hard life.

Reader 5: She told the United Nations something had to be done.

Reader 6: She made a list of rights for everyone.

Reader 1: I think she showed she cared.

Reader 2: And you're right on track.

All: Good ideas and acts make a hero.

Reader 3: And that's a fact!

Reader 4: Thomas Alva Edison was a smart guy.

Reader 5: He invented many things that people want to buy.

Reader 6: He made a phonograph and motion picture machine.

Reader 1: He showed moving pictures on a big white screen.

Reader 2: He made a lightbulb to light up the night.

Reader 3: He thought this would be useful and he was right.

Reader 4: I think he was smart.

Reader 5: And you're right on track.

All: Good ideas and acts make a hero.

Reader 6: And that's a fact!

Reader 1: A man named Cesar Chavez lent a helping hand.

Reader 2: He helped get better pay for those who farm the land.

Reader 3: Cesar worked hard to make the farm bosses change their ways.

Reader 4: Because of him, farmworkers have a better life these days.

Reader 5: I think Cesar showed courage.

Reader 6: And you're right on track.

Reader 1: And that's a fact!

Reader 2: In the world of Helen Keller, it was quiet and dark.

Reader 3: She couldn't see or speak, and this made her life very hard.

Reader 4: Annie Sullivan taught Helen when Helen was a girl.

Reader 5: Soon Helen could talk with her hands and learn about the world.

Reader 6: This story has two heroes.

Reader 1: And you're right on track!

All: Good ideas and acts made these heroes.

Reader 2: And that's a fact!

Reader 3: Dr. Martin Luther King, Jr., worked to improve our rights.

Reader 4: He used his words and fought with all his might.

Reader 5: He thought all people should be treated fairly, whatever their race.

Reader 6: Because of him our nation is a better place.

Reader 1: I think he showed courage.

Reader 2: And you're right on track.

All: Good ideas and acts make a hero.

Reader 3: And that's a fact!

Reader 4: Perhaps you know a hero who's alive today.

Reader 5: Maybe you know someone who acts in a special way.

Reader 6: Remember as you grow to keep yourself on track.

All: Good ideas and acts make a hero. And that's a fact!

The End

Simulations and Games

Who Am I? In a large box, gather together pictures or items that represent a variety of heroes. Examples include a lightbulb for Thomas Edison, a blueprint or a brick for Ieon Ming Pei, a sweet potato for George Washington Carver, and a microphone for Gloria Estefan. You may want to write the name of each hero represented on a notecard so children can figure out who is represented by the items in the box. Invite children to take turns as they select an item and act as the hero using this frame:

I am _____.

I am a hero because _____.

I helped others when I _____.

SIMULATION

Courage and Caring With the help of the children, draw several large circles on butcher paper to make a game board. Write one of these words in each of the circles: *courage, help, care.* Remind children that they can be heroes when they do brave things, help people, or show they care about others. Divide the class into groups, and provide each group with a game board and a beanbag. Have a player toss a beanbag onto one of the circles. The player reads the word and explains how they can do this action. For example, a child might say: *I show I care when I'm fair and share with others.* Have groups continue play until every child has had a turn. **GAME**

Dates In History   Have pairs of children play a game with a copy of a calendar. You will need one calendar per every two children. Fill in important historical dates on the calendar together as a class. Search the Internet using the keywords "This Day in History." Try to fill in as many dates as possible, such as Constitution Day on September 17.

The pairs will then play a game. First, the children will use black squares of construction paper to cover up all the dates on the calendar. The children will begin with the first date on the calendar. They will take turns trying to remember what happened on that date. The first player will say his or her answer, then look underneath the black square to see if he or she is correct. The child will do this without letting the other player see the answer.

If the child correctly guesses the event, he or she will uncover the date and advance to the next black square using a token. If the child incorrectly identifies the date, it is the other player's turn. If neither child answers correctly, the second child turns over the square covering the answer and both advance to the next square. The first player to get to the end of the calendar wins. **GAME**

Immigrant Box   Display an old suitcase. Divide the class into pairs. Ask partners to pretend they will be immigrants moving to a new country far away. They can only take those possessions that will fit into the suitcase. Invite children to make a list of the items they would choose to take with them. Invite partners to share their lists with the class. After each item, ask them to explain why they chose to take it. **SIMULATION**

5 Long-Term Project

CULTURAL FESTIVAL

Use this project to help children explore different world cultures.

Week 1 Introduce  class · 30 minutes

Materials: paper, pencils

Explain to the class that you will have a cultural festival in several weeks. Tell the children that this will give them the opportunity to share something with the class from one of the cultures around the world. Inform the children that those who have close ties to another world culture can share something from that culture. The rest of the children can pick a culture to share. Send a letter home with the children informing parents and guardians of your plans for the cultural festival and asking for their help.

Week 2 Plan individual · 30 minutes

Materials: writing paper, pencil

Give the children time to pick which culture they will share with the class. Help children who require assistance pick a culture. Then give children time to plan what they will share. Provide them with some options to consider, such as sharing a special cultural dish, a photograph of the country where the culture is located, or a book containing a story or artwork that has something to do with the culture they have selected. Other possibilities include a recording of an appropriate cultural song, a game, or a costume. Encourage the children to be creative and ask their parents or guardians for help.

Ask the children to write two sentences about what they plan to do. After the children have handed in their choices, review them for appropriateness and note any suggestions you might make to individual children to help them either consider sharing something else or narrowing the focus of what they plan to share. Make a list to use during the Week 3.

Week 3 Review

 class   60 minutes

Materials: supplies to make invitations, materials to set up festival, such as decorations or utensils

Spend some time reviewing all of the children's choices together as a class. Go down your list, mentioning what each child plans to share. Briefly discuss with the child what they have selected, making suggestions where appropriate.

Once you have reviewed the selections, determine with the class what you will need for the cultural festival. Answer questions such as: *Can we hold the festival in the classroom? What kinds of setup furniture do we need? Do we need utensils or plates for any food people might share? What kinds of decorations can we make to hang in the room?*

After you have figured out the setup for the festival, make any decorations you might have decided upon. Also ask the children to prepare a brief description (one or two sentences) of the cultural item they plan to share with the class.

Finally, have the children create invitations for parents, guardians, or other classes to the cultural festival.

Week 4 Festival!

 class   60 minutes

Materials: student-prepared materials

Hold the cultural festival. Make sure each child has time to briefly share with the class his or her contribution to the cultural festival. Have children take turns circulating around the room looking at whatever other children have brought to share. Encourage the children who are not circulating around the room to explain what they have brought to share to other children.

Tips for Combination Classrooms

 For Grade 1 students: Encourage children to recognize similarities and differences in cultural items shared by members of the class.

 For Grade 3 students: Encourage students to share a cultural item with significance for their family. Ask them to describe the significance.

UNIT
5 Short-Term Projects

Use these projects to help children explore culture and traditions.

Initial Biographies

 individual  30 minutes

Materials: Letters on 9″ × 12″ paper, crayons or markers

Give each child in the class the first letter of his or her name drawn the full size of a sheet of white 9″ × 12″ construction paper. It should be a block letter about $1\frac{1}{2}$″ wide. Children should use crayons or markers to decorate their letters by drawing things that represent traditions, customs, and celebrations that are special to them. Display the finished projects around the room. Have each child tell about his or her culture and traditions by explaining the items he or she chose to include on the initial.

Culture Collage

 individual   30 minutes

Materials: magazines, newspapers, drawing paper, scissors, glue or tape

Remind children that culture includes the attitudes, beliefs, and behaviors of a group of people. Then ask children to imagine that they have met someone who does not know anything about life in the United States. Have them create a collage of pictures from magazines and newspapers that illustrate aspects of American culture, such as food, clothing, art, beliefs, music, and language. Invite children to present their finished collage to the class and explain why they chose to include each image.

Class Quilt

Materials: photograph or self-portrait of each child, construction paper, tape or glue

Have children bring in a photograph of themselves or have them draw a self-portrait. Have them tape or glue their picture to a sheet of colored construction paper. Under their picture, have them write their name and something unique or special about themselves. Then ask the class to work together to attach all the pages to form a class "quilt." Display the quilt

and have a class discussion on diversity. Help children identify something special that each child contributes to the class.

Design a Medal

 partners · 30 minutes

Materials: examples of medals, pictures of heroes, ribbon or yarn, crayons or markers, drawing paper

Have children work in pairs to make a medal that honors a hero. Invite children to brainstorm words related to a hero's actions, such as *courage*, *compassion*, *caring*, *honesty*, or *hard work*. Suggest partners choose a hero and related action. Have them design a medal that shows the hero's portrait and names the action it honors. For example, the Medal of Courage might honor Jackie Robinson, or the Medal of Caring might honor Florence Nightingale. Staple each completed medal to a length of ribbon or thick yarn. Invite children to nominate classmates or school workers that might receive a medal during the course of the school year.

UNIT 5 Writing Projects

Use these prompts to help children explore different cultures and traditions.

A Journal Entry

 individual 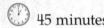 30 minutes

Have children imagine that they are immigrants who have just arrived in the United States. Invite them to write a journal entry describing their experiences in their new country. Ask them to include details such as where they came from, how they traveled to get here, and what customs from their home country they will keep.

Holiday Traditions

individual 45 minutes

Remind children that all families have traditions, or things they do year after year on special occasions. Have children write an expository paragraph describing their family's traditions and customs for a holiday or a special event such as a wedding or birthday. Ask them to include details about the roles different family members play, special food that is served, or costumes worn to celebrate the event.

Immigrant Interview

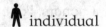 individual 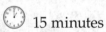 15 minutes

Have children create a list of questions to ask parents, grandparents, other relatives, or friends to find out why they immigrated to this country or moved to your community from a different state or neighborhood.

Moving On

 group 30 minutes

Have children work in small groups. Invite members of each group to choose a country they would like to move to as immigrants. Ask them to decide what they would take with them from their culture. Have them write a packing list and add a brief explanation of why they would choose to take each item.

A New Classmate

 class 30 minutes

Have children imagine that a new member of their class has just come from another country. Ask them what questions they could ask the new child about his or her culture. List the questions on the board.

What's in a Name?

 partners 30 minutes

Have children work in pairs to identify as many countries as they can that begin with the first letter of their first names. Have them find the countries on a map or a globe. Then have them list the names of the countries and the continents where they are located. Invite children to share their lists with the class.

Daily Geography

1. **Location**   Which state touches Kansas to the west?

2. **Location**   Which states do not touch any other states?

3. **Region**   In which region are most of the smaller states located?

4. **Place**   Of which state is Raleigh the capital?

5. **Place**   Of which state is Montgomery the capital?

6. **Place**   Of which state is Concord the capital?

7. **Movement**   In which direction would you travel from Washington to Oregon?

8. **Location**   Which of these states touches the Mississippi River?
Colorado
Arkansas
Maine

9. **Movement**   If you move goods from a factory in Rhode Island to a market in Connecticut, in which direction would you travel?

10. **Movement**   Imagine a truck is moving soybeans from Indiana to Nebraska and then to Texas. In which two directions will it travel?

11. **Movement**   Over which states would a plane pass if it flew in a straight line north from the middle of Texas to the middle of North Dakota?

12. **Location**   Which states would you start from and end with if you traveled from the capital city of Lincoln to the capital city of Des Moines?

13. **Place**   Of which state is Hartford the capital?

14. **Movement**   Which continent would an immigrant from India leave?

15. **Location**   On which continent is Ghana located?

16. **Place**   Which is the largest ocean in the world?

17. **Place**   Which country is the largest on the continent of North America?

18. **Location**   Which river is part of the border between the United States and Mexico?

19. **Movement**   Which ocean would a ship cross to get most quickly from North America to Australia?

20. **Movement**   Which ocean would a ship cross to get most quickly from Africa to North America?

21. **Location**   On which continent is El Salvador located?

22. **Location**   Which ocean is east of Africa and west of Australia?

23. **Location**   Which continent is west of South America and south of Asia?

24. **Location**   Which continent is west of North America and north of Australia?

25. **Movement**   In which direction would a plane travel if it flew from the center of Europe to the center of Africa?

26. **Movement**   In which direction would a plane travel if it flew from the center of South America to the center of Africa?

27. **Regions**   Which continent is the largest?

28. **Human-Environment Interactions**   If a truck carries lumber from Canada, in which of these cities might the truck first stop?
Phoenix, Arizona
Seattle, Washington
Wichita, Kansas

29. **Human-Environment Interactions**   If a truck carries vegetables from Mexico, in which of these cities might the truck first stop?
Little Rock, Arkansas
Butte, Montana
San Antonio, Texas

30. **Human-Environment Interactions**   If a ship brought fish from Alaska, in which city might it first dock?
Oakland, California
Tucson, Arizona
Miami, Florida

Why Character Counts

Respect

You show respect when you are nice to people who are different from you.

It is important to respect all people, not just people who look, act, or talk like you. Many people in the United States have moved here from other countries. They bring with them special traditions. Their traditions might be different from yours.

Learning about different traditions can help you respect other people. One way to learn about different traditions is to go to a festival.

In Your Own Words:

What does it mean to respect other people?

_____

_____

_____

_____

_____

Name _____

Character Activity

Interview someone in your class to learn more about his or her traditions. Use the questions below. Write your answers on the blank lines.

1. What is a tradition that is important to your family?

_____

_____

_____

2. Is there something in your family that has been passed down from your ancestors? What is it?

_____

_____

_____

3. Is there a special or favorite food that you eat in your family? If so, what does it taste like?

_____

_____

_____

Wants and Choices

All families have wants, or things they would like to have. They have to choose from these wants.

Rico Peralta and his family want to take an airplane trip to a family reunion in Mexico. Rico and his family also want a new computer. They cannot buy both airplane tickets and the computer now. What do they do?

Rico and his family decide to buy the airplane tickets. They do not want to miss the family reunion. They can save their money and buy a new computer later.

Name _____

Try It

Do these problems.

1. The Green family wants to buy new bikes. The Green family also likes to go to the amusement park every month. They cannot pay for both. What can they do?

_____

_____

_____

_____

_____

2. Callie is given $5 for her birthday. Callie wants new sunglasses. She also wants a new book. The sunglasses and the book each cost $5. What can she do?

_____

_____

_____

_____

_____

5 Citizenship

Read About It   Many people move to the United States for a better life and more freedom. The Declaration of Independence names some of the freedoms, or rights, that Americans enjoy. These rights protect people from unfair laws. They also give people the right to seek happiness. These rights cannot be taken away.

1. What are two freedoms, or rights, listed in the Declaration of Independence?

_____

_____

2. Why do many people move to the United States?

_____

_____

_____

Talk About It   The Declaration of Independence says that people have the right to seek happiness. What does this mean? Give an example of how one person's idea of happiness could stop another person from being happy. How does the government stop this from happening?

Name _____

Americans seek happiness in many different ways. How do you and your family seek happiness? Include at least three examples in your answer.

_____

_____

_____

_____

_____

_____

_____

_____

_____

_____

_____

Money Manager
Unit 6

Materials needed:

*Tape

*Scissors

*Drawing Paper

*Fine-tip markers or colored
  pencils

Social Studies Skills:

*History of Money

*Producers and Consumers

Reading Skills:

*Summarize

*Main Idea and Details

*Categorize

Instructions:

1. Copy the words and lines like
   those shown in the illustration.
   Fold along the dotted lines to
   make a wallet.

2. Tape the ends of the
   wallet closed.

3. Draw pictures and write
   information from
   the unit in each area.

Illustrations:

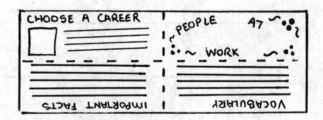

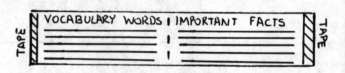

4. Design a new kind of money for your wallet with a picture in the middle and your own symbols on the bill. Be prepared to explain why you made these choices.

5. Make a credit card to put into your wallet.

6. Add other items to your wallet that you think people should carry with them.

Drama
ACTIVITY

Rocks of Gold

A readers theatre play about people in the marketplace

Cast of Characters

- Narrator 1
- Narrator 2
- Narrator 3
- Farmer
- Villager 1
- Villager 2
- Blacksmith
- Weaver
- Miller
- King

Narrator 1: Long ago there lived a farmer.

Narrator 2: He was a good, honest man, but he was very poor.

Farmer: I have a large piece of land, but I cannot farm it. It has far too many rocks.

Narrator 3: You see, every time he went to dig a hole, the farmer hit a rock. He had very rocky land.

Narrator 1: Every day the farmer kept digging.

Narrator 2: He made a pile of rocks.

Narrator 3: One day the farmer ran out of food.

Narrator 1: He decided to go to town.

Narrator 2: He came first to the blacksmith's shop.

Narrator 3: The blacksmith made tools, horseshoes, wagon wheels, and nails. He could trade his metal goods for food. He had plenty to eat.

Blacksmith: Hello, Farmer. How is your farm?

Farmer: It is full of rocks and not much else.

Blacksmith: You must be very hungry. Help me sweep out my shop and bring in wood. I will then share my lunch with you.

Narrator 1: So the poor farmer helped the blacksmith.

Narrator 2: They ate lunch together. Then the blacksmith gave the farmer a basket full of food.

Narrator 3: When the farmer had left, the blacksmith felt sorry for him.

Blacksmith: Poor farmer has nothing but rocks as his riches. He is a very poor man.

Narrator: After leaving the blacksmith's shop, the farmer walked down the street. Some of the villagers saw him.

Villager 1: Farmer, what do you have there?

Villager 2: Did you finally get your crops to grow?

Farmer: No, I got this food for working for the blacksmith.

Narrator 1: After a few days, the poor farmer was out of food again.

Narrator 2: Off he went to the village again. This time he met up with the weaver.

Weaver: Farmer, you are so thin and pale. Do you work too hard?

Farmer: I work very hard trying to find soil among all my rocks, but I can grow no food.

Weaver: Farmer, if you help me spin my yarn, I will fix you a fine supper.

Narrator 3: So the poor farmer helped the weaver spin and sew.

Narrator 1: They ate supper together. Then the weaver gave the farmer a box full of food. When the farmer had left, the weaver felt sorry for him.

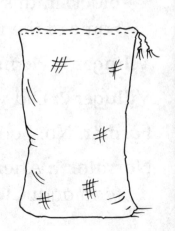

Weaver: That poor farmer has nothing but rocks as his riches. He is a very poor man indeed.

Narrator 2: After a few days, the farmer had again eaten all of his food.

Narrator 3: Bright and early, he set off for the village again. This time he went to visit the miller.

Miller: Farmer, I am glad you are here. Can you help me grind grain into flour? Then we will eat a meal.

Narrator 1: So the farmer helped the miller.

Narrator 2: After work, they ate breakfast together. Then the miller gave the farmer a bag of grain.

Narrator 1: Some villagers saw the farmer in the street.

Villager 1: Oh farmer, I see you have been helping again!

Villager 2: If only someone needed your crop of rocks.

Narrator 3: One day, the king arrived in the village.

King: I want to build a big castle with strong walls made from stones and rocks.

Villagers 1 and 2: We know just the person you are looking for!

Narrator 1: The villagers showed the king to the farmer's house.

King: I understand you are the man to see about rocks for my castle.

Narrator 2: The farmer had so many rocks for the king that the castle was built in no time at all.

Narrator 3: The king paid the farmer for the rocks with many bags of gold.

Farmer: I guess my rocks were my riches. Now I am a very rich man!

The End

UNIT 6 Simulations and Games

Assembly Line   Help children imagine they are workers on an assembly line in a factory. Give small groups an assembled toy such as a model car, a board game, or a stuffed animal. Point out that each worker in a factory is responsible for attaching or putting together one part. Have children decide on a job for each member to do to assemble the toy. Have groups pretend to assemble the toy and narrate their job as it "moves down the line." Invite groups to present their assembly line for the class. **SIMULATION**

Trade Charades   Divide the class into groups. Help each group make a set of cards that name a country and one product it trades to the United States on each card. Put all the cards in a pile. Have children take turns drawing a card, naming the country, and pantomiming the product as the group guesses what it is. For example, for maple syrup from Canada, a child names the country and pantomimes pouring maple syrup over and eating a stack of pancakes. **GAME**

Shopping Trip   Have small groups pretend they are going on a shopping trip downtown or in a mall. Ask them to tell what businesses they would visit and what goods or services they might buy at each business. **SIMULATION**

I Have, You Want   Divide the class into small groups. One group member starts game play by naming a job and telling whether it provides a good or service. For example: I am a dentist and I provide a service. The next player answers as a consumer and tells a specific good or service they get from the producer. For example: I am a consumer and I want to have my teeth cleaned. The same player then names a new job and whether they produce a good or service and play continues. **GAME**

Let's Go Shopping   Invite children to set up a "store" by making price tags and labeling a variety of classroom objects and school supplies. Have children use play money to practice buying and selling goods in the store. Divide the class into two groups, one to buy and one to sell the goods. Ask the groups to trade places so each group has a chance to "shop." **SIMULATION**

Goods Matching Game   Help groups of children prepare cards for a matching game. Give each group member four cards. Ask each child to write on each of their cards the name of a person that makes or sells goods and two examples of goods that they sell. Examples include baker: bread, muffins; florist: flowers, vase; bookseller: books, newspapers; or clothing store: sweaters, socks. Have each group mix up their cards. Explain that one child should deal four cards to each player. The remaining cards are placed facedown in the center. Players take turns drawing from their neighbor or the pile, discarding sets as they are made. **GAME**

TOWN SHOPS MODEL

**Use this project to help children think more in depth about how
communities produce and use goods and services.**

Week 1   Introduce
 group   30 minutes

Materials: paper, pencils

Introduce the project by asking questions such as: *When you shop with your
family, what stores do you visit? Where does your family shop often? Which stores
have special things you want to buy?* Invite children to name goods and services
their family buys and list them on the board.

Tell children that they will use art materials to build a model of an
imaginary downtown shopping district where people go to buy things.
Divide the class into groups. Ask each group to make a list of stores they
think the town should have, using these questions: *Where will families buy
goods or services they need, such as food, clothing, medicine, heat, and power? What
stores will sell goods that people use at school or work? What stores will sell goods we
want, such as sports equipment, videos and music, toys, and pet supplies? What stores
will provide services such as haircuts or car repair?*

Have groups share their lists with the class. Explain that each child will
choose and make a model of a store and decide what goods or services he or
she will provide. Encourage children to avoid choosing a "mega-store" and
instead choose a store that features a specialty such as a bakery, an auto
supply, or a hardware store. Make a chart that lists children's choices so there
is a variety of store types.

Week 2 Plan

 group   30 minutes

Materials: paper, pencils, drawing paper, crayons or markers

Have children work in small groups to plan how they will build their stores. Suggest each "store owner" make a list of goods or services they will provide. Ask each child to make an ad that can be displayed to advertise their store and its goods or services.

Week 3 Construct

 group   45 minutes

Materials: small boxes, milk cartons, glue, art supplies, crayons or markers, construction paper

Provide each child with a small box or clean, empty milk carton. Explain that they can use this as their store building. Ask them to cover the box or carton with paper to make it look like a store, drawing in doors and windows and adding a sign to the front. Suggest that they draw a display for the window so people will want to come inside. Assist children as they form their stores into a downtown shopping district. Have them use construction paper to add roads, sidewalks, and trees.

Week 4 Present

 group   30 minutes

Plan a day for children to present their shops. Allow each child time to identify their store and tell about what they sell. Invite other children to ask questions.

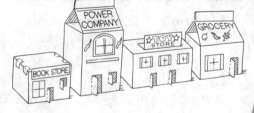

Tips for Combination Classrooms

1-2 **For Grade 1 students:** Have children draw and label a simple map of the town, including cardinal directions and map symbols for each store.

2-3 **For Grade 3 students:** Ask children to write sentences about how natural resources are used for the goods or services provided by certain stores.

UNIT 6 Short-Term Projects

Use these projects to help children explore how people interact in the marketplace.

Store Graph

 group   45 minutes

Materials: drawing paper, crayons or markers

Have children make up the number of goods sold in a store and then use the information to make a bar graph. Working in small groups, have children choose a store. Have groups choose five goods the store might sell and decide how many of each item were sold in a week, using numbers from 1 to 10. Have them use the information to make a bar graph that shows the amounts of each item sold at the store.

The Music Store

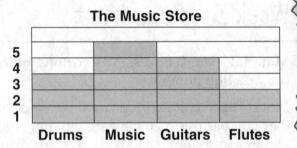

Drums	Music	Guitars	Flutes

5 4 3 2 1

From Factory to You

 partners   45 minutes

Materials: research materials, index cards, string, tape, crayons or markers

Help pairs research how a factory product such as a toy, a machine, or a food product is made. Children may find these books helpful: *Wax to Crayons* by Inez Snyder; *Tomatoes to Ketchup* by Inez Snyder; *How Things Are Made: From Automobiles to Zippers* by Sharon Rose and Neil Schlager.

Invite pairs to draw pictures on index cards that show each step used to make a product. Have them attach the cards in order with string and tape to form a hanging flowchart.

Worldwide Trade

Materials: drawing paper, pencils, crayons or markers

Our country trades goods with other countries to get products we like to buy. Invite children to make a list of items in their household that come from other countries. Suggest that children look at labels, tags, directions, and words on the products that tell where they came from. Have groups use the lists to make a table that shows the products we get from other countries. Have them write the names of four countries down the left side of the table. Using their lists, ask groups to draw pictures of products they found for each country in the row next to the country's name.

Germany		
Mexico		
China		
Japan		

Produce and Consume

Materials: construction paper, mail-order catalogs, paste, scissors, crayons or markers

Invite children to work in small groups to make a poster that shows producers and consumers of a product. Ask groups to look through catalogs for an interesting product and cut out its picture. Have them paste the picture to the top of a sheet of construction paper and draw a line down the center to divide the paper in half. Next, ask each group member to draw either a picture of a person making or selling the product, or a person buying or using the product. Have groups cut out and paste their pictures on the poster so that the left side shows producers and the right side shows consumers.

UNIT 6 Writing Projects

Use these prompts to get children writing about the marketplace and spending money.

Where Does Money Go? individual 30 minutes

Have children make an accordion book about using money. Cut large sheets of drawing paper into strips. Have each child fold a strip accordion-style into four sections. Ask them to write this title in the first section: *Where Does Money Go?* In each remaining section, invite children to write a sentence that tells how they or their family members spend money, save money, and share money. Ask children to illustrate their books.

A Good Job for Me individual 30 minutes

Ask children to write a journal entry that explains a job they would like to do when they are adults. Tell the children that people sometimes pick jobs because of things they like to do, talents they have, or the places where they live. Suggest that children think about these common concerns as they write. Invite children to share their journal entries with the class.

Start a Business partners 30 minutes

Ask children to imagine that they will start a new business. Have them work together in pairs to write a paragraph about the new business. Examples of businesses could be age-appropriate, such as a lemonade stand, or imagined, such as an Internet company.

Likeable Labels

 partners   30 minutes

Invite children to share their favorite vegetables and discuss why it is important that we buy and eat these vegetables. Display various empty packages of canned, frozen, or fresh vegetables as examples. Ask pairs of children to design a package for a favorite vegetable. Remind them that the package needs to get buyers' attention, give information about the vegetable, and tell buyers why it is important that they buy the vegetable. Display the finished labels on a bulletin board.

People at Work

 group   30 minutes

In advance, gather together magazine and newspaper pictures of people at work in various jobs. Ask children to compare the pictures and sort them into types of work, such as *people who keep us healthy*, *people who work with children*, or *people who make goods*. Divide the class into groups. Give each group a set of pictures. Ask group members to write captions for each picture and arrange the captions and pictures to make a poster. Suggest they use the type of work depicted as the title for their poster.

To the Store

 class   15 minutes

Help the class write an imaginary story about how a product might get from a country far away to the children's community. Display a world map. Name a product that is imported to the United States from a country far away, such as fabric from Nepal, wool from Mongolia, glassware from Austria, or leather from Argentina. Help children find the location on the map. Then invite children to take turns using the map and creating a sentence that tells a small part of the product's journey. For example, they might say: *Glasses are on trucks from the factory in Austria to Germany. The glass moves by train from Germany to France. Then it goes by boat from France to New York. Finally it moves by truck to our community.* Remind them to identify the transportation used and choose a place for each part of the voyage to begin and to end. Write the story on the board as it is developed.

6 Daily Geography

1. **Place**	Which city is the state capital of Nevada?
2. **Location**	Which state touches South Dakota to the south?
3. **Location**	Which states touch Tennessee to the north?
4. **Place**	Which of these states has a capital city named for a President? Maine Nebraska South Dakota
5. **Movement**	In which direction would an explorer travel if he went from South Carolina to West Virginia?
6. **Location**	Which state is west of the Mississippi River? Kentucky Indiana Missouri
7. **Movement**	In which direction would a pilot fly if she flew from Utah to Missouri?
8. **Place**	Which state is Jackson the capital of?
9. **Place**	Which two state names have another state's one-word name in them?
10. **Location**	Which of the Great Lakes is the only one completely in the United States?
11. **Location**	Which states touch Florida to the north?
12. **Place**	Which city is the capital of New Mexico?
13. **Location**	Which states touch Idaho to the west?
14. **Place**	Which state is Jefferson City the capital of?
15. **Place**	What is the capital of Georgia?

16. Place   Thomas Edison was born in Ohio. What is the capital city of this state?

17. Place   Astronaut Sally Ride was born in Los Angeles, the biggest city in California. What is the capital of the state?

18. Location   Which states form the borders of New Jersey?

19. Location   What is the name of the island on which the capital city of Hawaii is found?

20. Movement   An inventor in Indianapolis, Indiana, takes her invention to Washington, D.C. In which direction does she travel?

21. Movement   What are the names of the states you would travel through if you went from Louisiana to South Carolina?

22. Place   Cesar Chavez was born in Arizona. What is the capital city of this state?

23. Human-Environment Interactions   In which of these cities in the United States could you see fishing boats on the ocean?
Charleston, South Carolina
Denver, Colorado
Harrisburg, Pennsylvania

24. Location   On which continent is India?

25. Regions   Which of these states is in the northeast part of the United States?
Louisiana
Utah
Massachusetts

26. Regions   Which of these states is in the southwest part of the United States?
Alabama
Arizona
Wisconsin

27. Location   Which continents are completely north of the equator?

28. Location   Which continents are completely south of the equator?

29. Location   Which continent is south of North America and west of Africa?

30. Location   Which continent is east of South America and west of Australia?

Why Character Counts

Trustworthiness

Trustworthiness means you say or do things that make people trust you. Being trustworthy means that you tell the truth, follow rules, and do what you say you will do. Trustworthy people do not take things that do not belong to them.

When people sell goods, they need to be trustworthy. If a store sells you a toy or game, you expect it to work and not break. You also expect the store to sell goods at a fair price.

✓ **Trustworthiness**
- **Respect**
- **Responsibility**
- **Fairness**
- **Caring**
- **Patriotism**

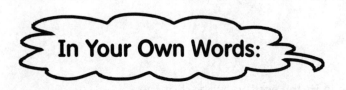

In Your Own Words:

What does it mean to be trustworthy?

_____

_____

_____

_____

Name _____

Character Activity

Answer the following questions.

1. Josh is riding his bike to school. He thinks about a new book he wants to buy. Then Josh sees a wallet on the ground. He looks around, but he sees no one is nearby. Josh opens the wallet. Inside he finds a person's address and some money. How can Josh show he is trustworthy?

_____

_____

_____

_____

2. Tell about a time you showed your family you were trustworthy. What did you say or do to help your family trust you?

_____

_____

_____

_____

UNIT 6 Economic Literacy

Cost of Goods

Some goods cost more than others. Some goods cost less. The cost of goods depends on how many of the goods are for sale. It also depends on how many people want to buy that good.

There is a new computer for sale in stores. You would like one. Many other children want one. The price is high. Why?

The price is high because everyone wants one. When a lot of people want the same thing, the price goes up. People are willing to pay a higher price.

There is a store that sells sweaters from Central America. Each sweater is made by hand with special wool. It takes a long time to make each sweater, so there are not many for sale. Each sweater costs a lot. Do you know why?

The price is high because there are not many to buy.

Try It

Do these problems.

1. The toy stores have a new radio-controlled car for sale. There are lots of ads for the car. Many people want to buy the car. Will the price for this car be high or low? Why?

_____

_____

2. Six months go by. The radio-controlled car is not new anymore. Some people already bought one. Other people no longer want it. There are plenty of cars to buy, but few people want them. What will happen to the price of the car? Why?

_____

_____

_____

6 Citizenship

> **Read About It** In the United States, people vote to choose their leaders. They vote for someone who they think will do a good job as a leader. To vote in an election, people have to be citizens of the United States. They also have to be at least 18 years old. They must also follow certain rules such as signing up to vote before the election.

1. Why do people in the United States vote?

_____

_____

2. Who can vote in an election in the United States?

_____

_____

_____

> **Talk About It** In the past, only certain people were allowed to vote in elections. The Constitution was changed so that women and people of any race or color could vote. Why is it fair that all citizens have the same right to vote? What would it be like if only certain groups of people could vote for our leaders?

Name _____

> **Write About It**   A vote is a way to let people know what you want. A vote is a choice that gets counted. Even if you are not old enough to vote in elections, you can make other choices by voting. Create a story where the main characters vote to make a decision.

_____

_____

_____

_____

_____

_____

_____

_____

_____

_____

_____

_____

Location

Where is a place located?

What is it near?

What direction is it from another place?

Why are certain features or places located where they are?

Place

What is it like there?

What physical and human features does it have?

The Five Themes of Geography

Human-Environment Interactions

How are people's lives shaped by the place?

How has the place been shaped by people?

Regions

How is this place like other places?

What features set this place apart from other places?

Movement

How did people, products, and ideas get from one place to another?

Why do they make these movements?

Social Studies Journal

The most important thing I learned was . . .

Something that I did not understand was . . .

What surprised me the most was . . .

I would like to know more about . . .

K	What I **K**now

W	What I **W**ant to Know

L	What I **L**earned

Main Idea and Supporting Details

Supporting Detail	Supporting Detail

⇨ **Main Idea** ⇦

Supporting Detail	Supporting Detail

Fact and Opinion

Fact	Opinion
✓ **Fact**	✗ **Opinion**
✓ **Fact**	✗ **Opinion**
✓ **Fact**	✗ **Opinion**
✓ **Fact**	✗ **Opinion**

Cause and Effect

Effect

Cause

Compare and Contrast

Information About "A"	Information About "B"

Categorize

Sequence

Event

	Order

Event

Event

Event

Event

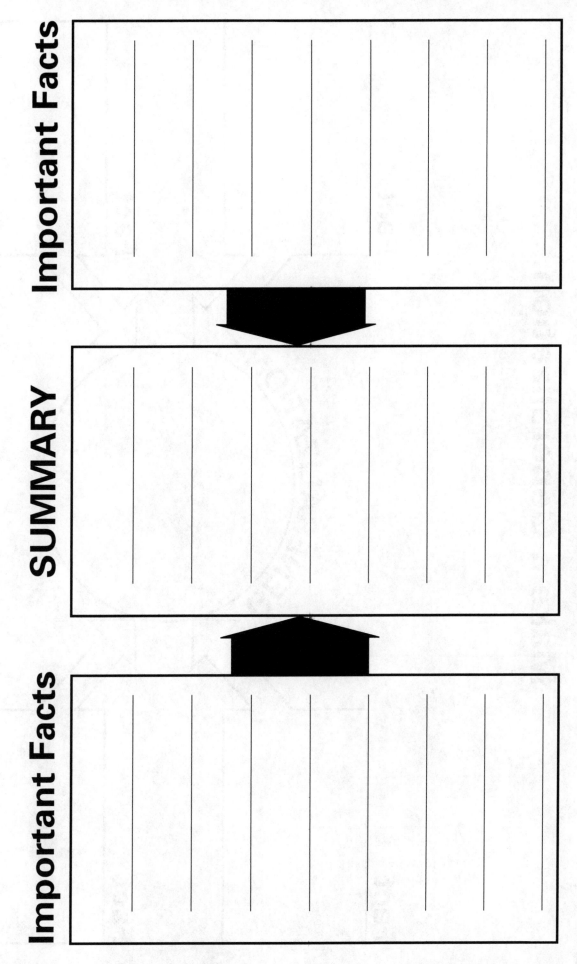

Summarize

Important Facts

SUMMARY

Important Facts

Make a Generalization

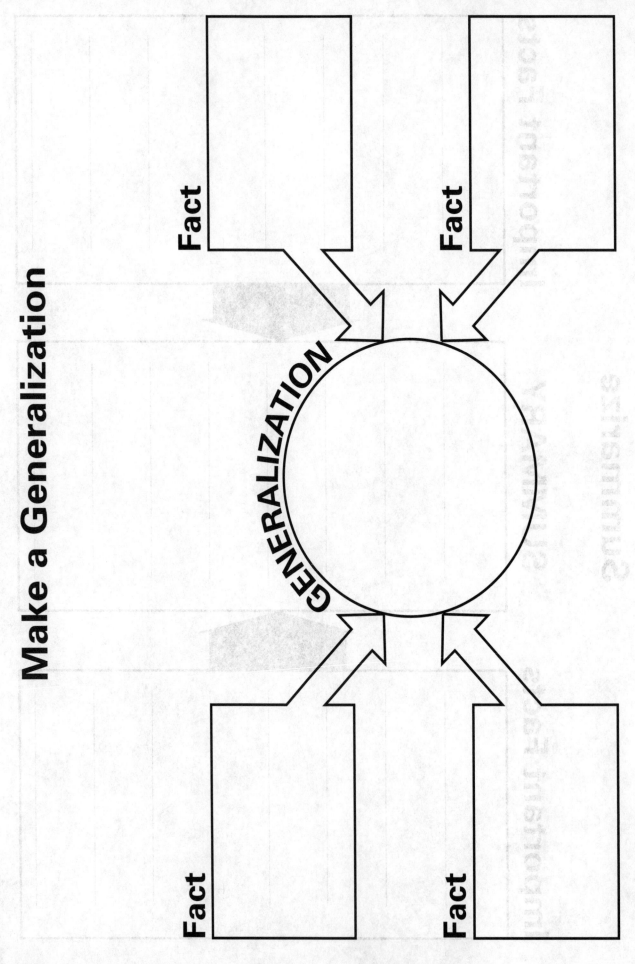

Fact

Fact

GENERALIZATION

Fact

Fact

Draw a Conclusion

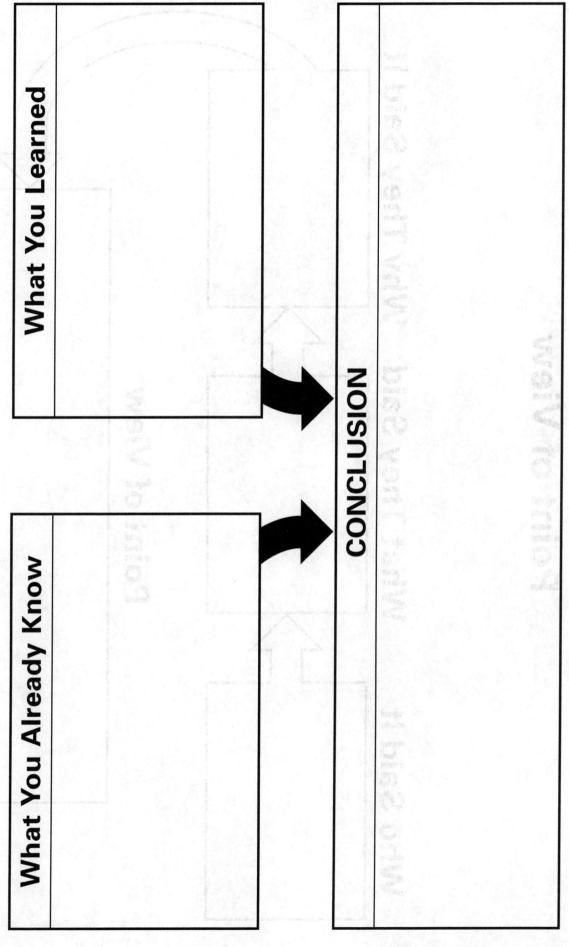

What You Learned

What You Already Know

CONCLUSION

Point of View

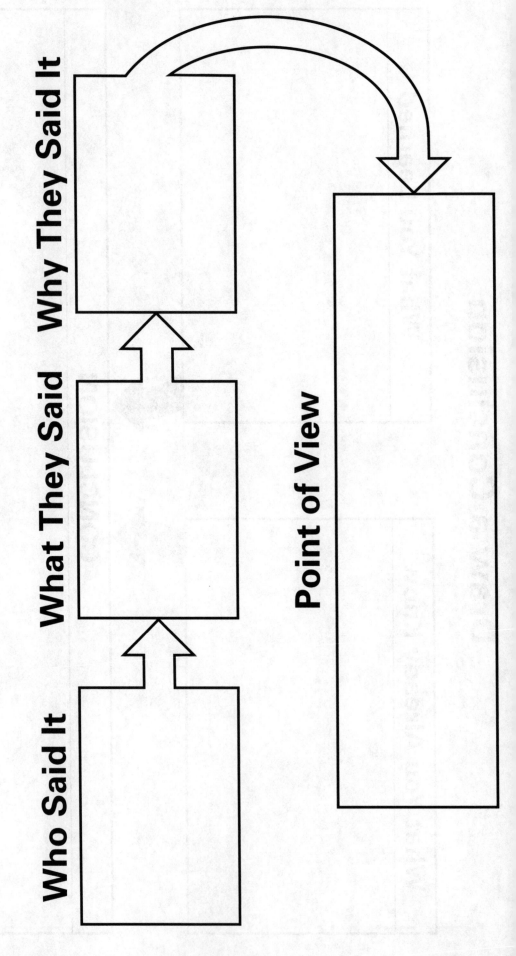

Why They Said It

What They Said

Who Said It

Point of View

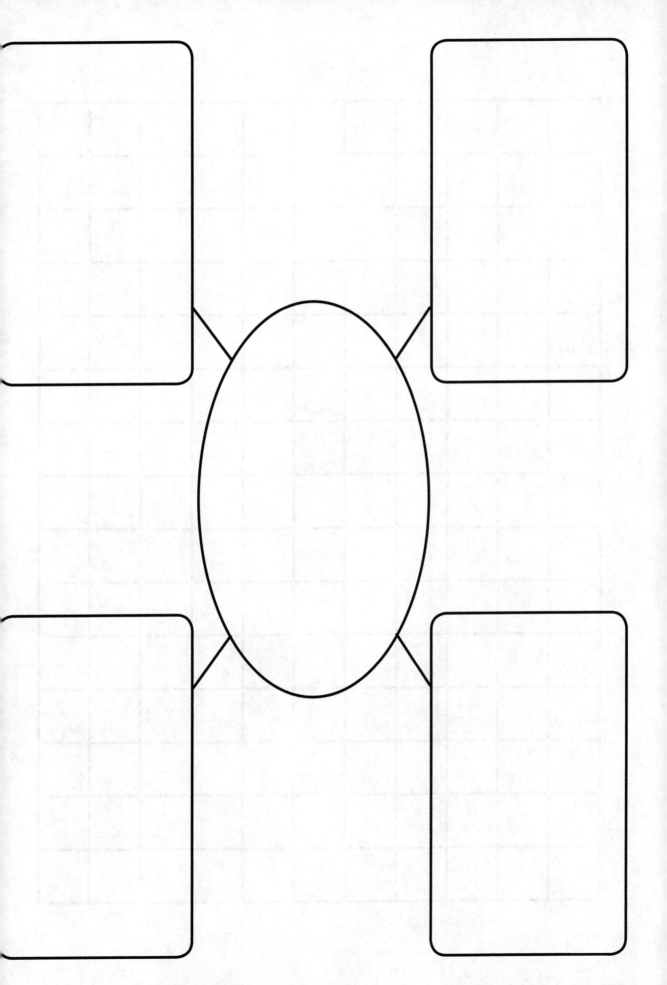

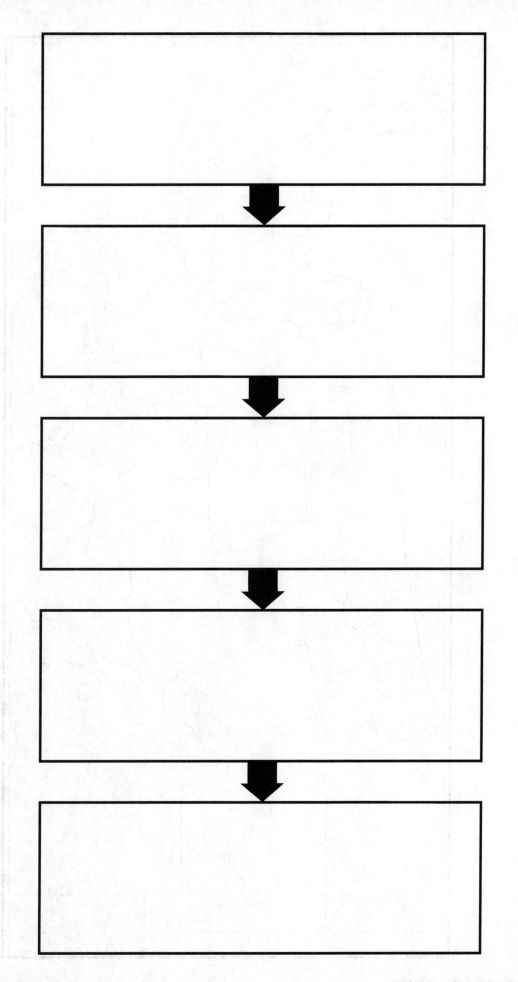

The United States

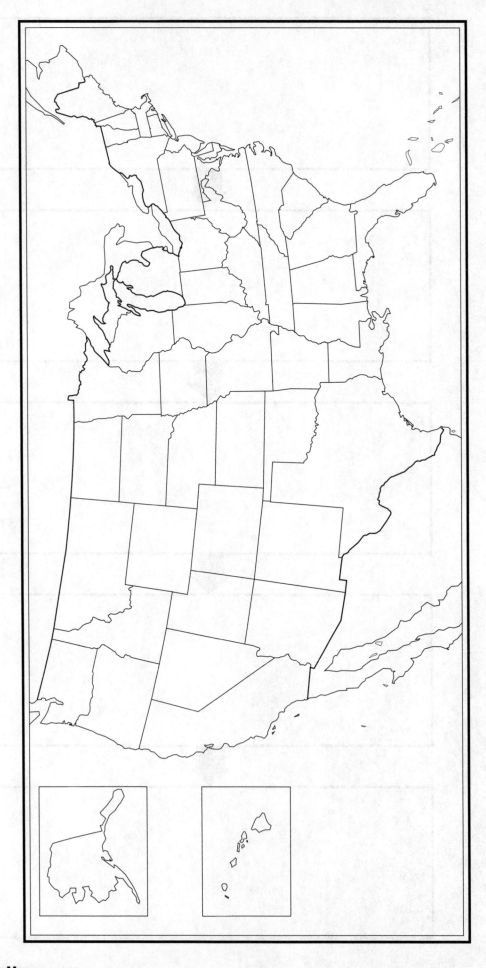

North America

The World

Eastern Hemisphere

Western Hemisphere

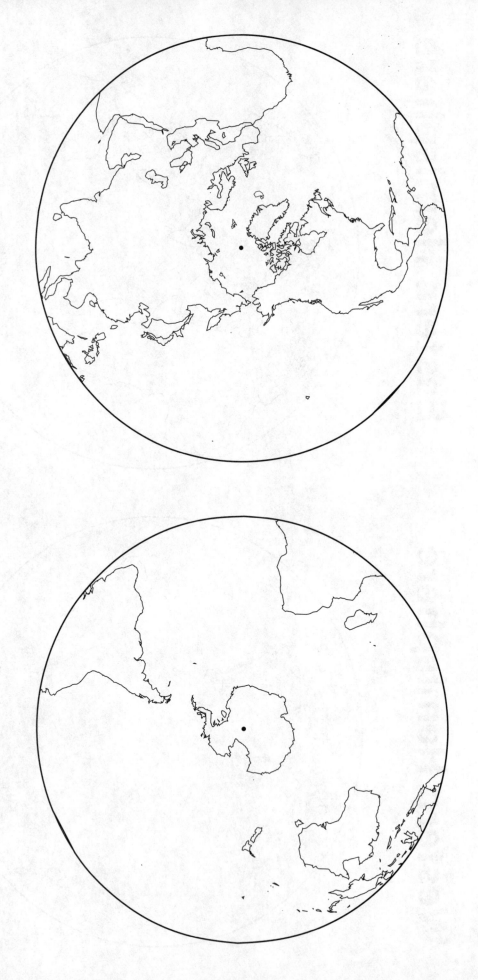

Northern Hemisphere

Southern Hemisphere

Planning Options

♦ individual   ♦♦ partners   ♦♦♦ group/class

	Activity	Materials	🕐	Link	
Drama Activity pages 6–9	**A Student Government Team** Children read a readers theatre about running for student government.		45 min.	U1, Les. 1–3	♦♦♦
Simulations and Games pages 10–11	**Democracy Dominoes** Children play dominoes using government terminology.	index cards, pencils	30 min.	U1	♦♦♦
	Island Government Children set up rules for living on a deserted island.	paper, pencils	45 min.	U1, Les. 1–2	♦♦♦
	Voting Day Children simulate activities that take place on Election Day.		20 min.	U1, Les. 3	♦♦♦
	Press Conference Children role-play a press conference about the government.	index cards, pencils	30 min.	U1, Les. 4–5	♦♦
	Make a Pair Children review the role and jobs of government entities or people.	index cards	20 min.	U1, Les. 3–5	♦♦♦
Long-Term Project pages 12–13	**A Local Government Directory**			U1, Les. 5	♦♦♦
	Week 1 Children are introduced to the project and begin to compile a list of local officials.	paper, pencils	30 min.		
	Week 2 Children research the biographies and responsibilities of local officials.	paper, pencils, research materials	45 min.		
	Week 3 Children put together their directories.	drawing paper, crayons or markers, construction paper, glue or tape, hole punch, yarn	45 min.		
	Week 4 Children present and display their finished directories.	display area for directories, camera (optional)	15 min.		

	Activity	Materials	🕐	Link	
Short-Term Projects pages 14–15	**In the News** Children find and classify articles about our government at work.	newspaper, news magazines, poster-board, scissors, tape or glue	30 min.	U1, Les. 4	
	Successful Student Rule Book Children write rules to be a successful student.	drawing paper, crayons or markers, construction paper, hole punch, yarn	45 min.	U1, Les. 2	
	Our Government at Work Children create posters for government projects for the community.	posterboard, crayons or markers, scissors, newspapers and magazines, glue	30 min.	U1, Les. 2	
	Presidential Trading Cards Children create trading cards of the United States Presidents.	research materials, drawing paper, crayons or markers	30 min.	U1, Les. 3	
Writing Projects pages 16–17	**Election Night Speech** Children write speeches.	paper, pencils	30 min.	U1, Les. 4	
	Groups and Leaders Children create lists of all the different groups they belong to and identify the leader of each group.	paper, pencils	20 min.	U1, Les. 2	
	Dear City Council Children write letters to the city council.	paper, pencils	30 min.	U1, Les. 5	
	Laws and Consequences Children create laws with consequences.	paper, pencils	30 min.	U1, Les. 1	
	Choose by Voting Children use voting to make a choice and write about the experience.	paper, pencils	30 min.	U1, Les. 3	
Why Character Counts pages 20–21	**Fairness** Students read about fairness and complete a follow-up activity.	pencils	40 min.	U1, Les. 1	
Economic Literacy pages 22–23	**Services and Volunteers** Children read about services and volunteers and complete a follow-up activity.	pencils	30 min.	U1, Les. 2	
Citizenship pages 24–25	**The Constitution** Children read about the Constitution and complete a writing activity.	pencils	45 min.	U1, Les. 4	

UNIT 2 Planning Options

individual   partners   group/class

	Activity	Materials	🕐	Link	
Drama Activity pages 28–31	**A Secret Map** Children read a readers theatre play about the land and maps.		30 min.	U2, Les. 1	group/class
Simulations and Games pages 32–33	**How Do I Get There From Here?** Children give directions using maps and directional terms.	map of the United States	30 min.	U2, Les. 1, 4	partners
	Landform Tag Children play tag using clues about landforms.		20 min.	U2, Les. 2	group/class
	Where Is It? Children use cardinal directions to give one another clues.	bean bag	20 min.	U2, Les. 4	group/class
	Crazy Locations Children play a matching geography game.	index cards	30 min.	U2, Les. 1–2	group/class
	Seasons Charades Children play charades with words about seasons, climate, and weather.	paper	30 min.	U2, Les. 4	group/class
Long-Term Project pages 34–35	**3-D Maps of the Land** **Week 1** Introduce the project. Children will create three-dimensional maps.	large sheets of cardboard, paper, pencils	30 min.	U2, Les. 2	group/class
	Week 2 Children plan their maps.	craft paper, pencils, modeling clay, paint, assorted toys, recycled materials	30 min.		
	Week 3 Children make their maps.	art materials, paint, markers, labels	60 min.		
	Week 4 Children present their maps.	display space, camera (optional)	30 min.		

	Activity	Materials	🕐	Link	
Short-Term Projects pages 36–37	**Continental Capitals** Children complete an untitled map of North America.	outline map of North America, reference materials, crayons or colored pencils	30 min.	U2, Les. 2	
	Playground Map Students design their ideal playground.	paper, pencils, crayons or markers	30 min.	U2, Les. 1	
	Land Brochures Students create a brochure of their community's landforms.	community or city maps, local newspapers or brochures, drawing paper, crayons or markers	45 min.	U2, Les. 2	
	Make a Mural Children make a mural illustrating one scene in each season.	butcher paper, crayons or markers	30 min.	U2, Les. 3	
Writing Projects pages 38–39	**Local Climate** Children describe local climate.	paper, pencils	30 min.	U2, Les. 3	
	Compare and Contrast Landforms Children use a Venn diagram to compare and contrast landforms.	paper, pencils	30 min.	U2, Les. 2	
	Map Key Riddles Children write riddles about map symbols.	paper, pencils	30 min.	U2, Les. 2	
	Absolute and Relative Directions Children write directions using absolute and relative locations.	paper, pencils	30 min.	U2, Les. 1	
	State Brochures Children create brochures about their state.	paper, pencils	60 min.	U2, Les. 4	
Why Character Counts pages 42–43	**Patriotism** Students read about patriotism and complete a follow-up activity.	pencils	40 min.	U2, Les. 1	
Economic Literacy pages 44–45	**Making Money** Students read about earning money and complete a follow-up activity.	pencils	30 min.	U6, Les. 1	
Citizenship Pages 46–47	**The Bill of Rights** Students read about private property and complete a writing activity.	pencils	45 min.	U1, Les. 4	

Planning Options

individual   partners   group/class

	Activity	Materials	🕐	Link	
Drama Activity pages 50–53	**The Root Cellar** Children read a readers theatre play about using the land's resources, today and long ago.		45 min.	U3, Les. 1	
Simulations and Games pages 54–55	**Transportation Alphabet** Children play a word game by naming different forms of transportation.		20 min.	U3, Les. 4	
	Farming Past and Present Children compare different tasks from the past and the present.	index cards	45 min.	U3, Les. 3	
	We Use Resources Children review the use of natural resources.	index cards	20 min.	U3, Les. 1	
	Recycling Inventions Children use recycled products in a new way.	various recyclable objects	30 min.	U3, Les. 1	
	World Travelers Children hone their geography skills using a globe.	world globe	15 min.	U3, Les. 4	
Long-Term Project pages 56–57	**Farming Bulletin Board**			U3, Les 1, 3	
	Week 1 Children compare farming in the past to farming in the present.	paper, pencils	30 min.		
	Week 2 Children draw pictures for the bulletin board.	research materials, drawing paper, pencils, markers or crayons, scissors, butcher paper	30 min.		
	Week 3 Children glue their drawings to the board and write related captions.	art supplies, glue, bulletin board space, stapler	60 min.		
	Week 4 Children discuss the final bulletin board.		30 min.		

	Activity	Materials	🕐	Link	
Short-Term Projects pages 58–59	**Geography Poster** Students sort pictures of landforms and bodies of water.	old magazines, newspapers, construction paper, glue, scissors, crayons or markers.	30 min.	U3, Les. 2	
	Charting Map Symbols Students compare different map symbols.	maps, paper, pencils	30 min.	U3, Les. 2	
	Favorite Farm Produce Children create a picture graph of their favorite farm products.	paper, pencils, crayons or markers	30 min.	U3, Les. 1, 3	
	Air, Water, and Land Children create a poster to illustrate our use of natural resources.	construction paper, crayons or markers	45 min.	U3, Les. 1	
Writing Projects pages 60–61	**A Journey** Children create travelogues.	state map, paper, pencils	45 min.	U3, Les. 4	
	Dear Friend Children describe housing in different environments.	photographs of homes, paper, pencils	30 min.	U3, Les. 2	
	Plan a Resource Field Trip Children plan a field trip.	paper, pencils, research materials	30 min.	U3, Les. 1	
	Recycle and Conserve Children create posters telling others to recycle and conserve.	paper, pencils, markers or crayons	30 min.	U3, Les. 1	
	Letter to the Editor Children write about the environment.	paper, pencils	30 min.	U3, Les. 1	
	Conservation Brochure Children create a brochure about recycling and conservation.	paper, pencils, markers or crayons	30 min.	U3, Les. 3	
Why Character Counts pages 64–65	**Caring** Students read about caring and complete a follow-up activity.	pencils	40 min.	U3, Les. 1	
Economic Literacy pages 66–67	**Make a Budget** Students read about budgeting and complete a follow-up activity.	pencils	30 min.	U6, Les. 2	
Citizenship Pages 68–69	**Laws and Rights** Children read about laws and rights and complete a writing activity.	pencils	45 min.	U1 Les. 1	

Planning Options

♦ individual   **♦♦** partners   **♦♦♦** group/class

	Activity	Materials	🕐	Link	
Drama Activity pages 72–75	**The Old Jacket** Children read a readers theatre play about families and the past.		45 min.	U4, Les. 1	♦♦♦
Simulations and Games pages 76–77	**Pick-a-Word Relay** Children play a relay game with vocabulary words.	index cards	20 min.	U4	♦♦♦
	Grid-Tac-Toe Children play tic-tac-toe on a grid with national landmarks.	index cards, postcards of national landmarks, checkers, posterboard	30 min.	U4, Les. 4	♦♦
	Signing the Declaration of Independence Children simulate signing the Declaration of Independence.	posterboard or large paper, markers or pencils	30 min.	U4, Les. 3	♦♦♦
	The Native American Hand Game Children play a Native American guessing game.	two buttons or small stones, ten counting sticks, such as toothpicks or chenille sticks	20 min.	U4, Les. 2	♦♦♦
	Revolutionary War Time Line Challenge Children place events leading up to the Revolutionary War in chronological order.	sentence strips	20 min.	U4 Les. 3	♦♦♦
Long-Term Project pages 78–79	**A Biography Quilt** **Week 1** Children collect information about a chosen hero.	paper, pencils, resource materials	30 min.		♦♦♦
	Week 2 Children draw their quilt squares and write captions.	6-inch squares of construction paper, pencils, crayons or markers	30 min.		
	Week 3 Children construct the quilt.	butcher paper, glue, markers or crayons	30 min.		
	Week 4 Children display the quilts.	hanging space for display, camera (optional)	30 min.		

	Activity	Materials	🕐	Link	
Short-Term Projects pages 124–125	**Long Ago and Yesterday** Children create picture pairs to show yesterday or long ago.	construction paper, resource materials, crayons, markers	45 min.	U4, Les. 1–2	👥👤👤
	Washington, D.C. Landmarks Children review Washington, D.C. landmarks and draw a picture of one of them.	pictures of Washington, D.C. landmarks, drawing paper, crayons	30 min.	U4, Les. 4	👤
	Hero Mystery Box Children gather items representing the work and life of a hero.	shoeboxes, art supplies, crayons or markers	30 min.	U4, Les. 5	👥👤👤
	Make a Monument Children design a monument for a hero of their choosing.	resource books and photographs of monuments, paper, pencils, craft supplies	45 min.	U4, Les. 4	👥👤👤
Writing Projects pages 82–83	**Interview Questions** Children write interview questions for Revolutionary War heroes.	paper, pencils	30 min.	U4, Les. 3	👥👤
	Symbols of Our Nation Children describe a landmark.	paper, pencils, pictures of Washington, D.C., landmarks	45 min.	U4, Les. 4	👤
	My Hero Children write a poem about an everyday hero.	paper, pencils	15 min.	U4, Les. 5	👤
	A Ship's Log Children write an entry in a ship's log.	paper, pencils	30 min.	U4, Les. 2	👤
	Riddles of the Past Children write riddles about old tools.	paper, pencils, various utensils	30 min.	U4, Les. 1, 2	👥👤👤
	Write a Journal Children write journal entries.	paper, pencils	45 min.	U4, Les. 1	👥👤👤
Why Character Counts Pages 86–87	**Responsibility** Children read about responsibility and complete a follow-up activity.	pencils	40 min.	U4, Les. 5	👤
Economic Literacy pages 88–89	**Producers and Consumers** Children read about producers and consumers and complete a follow-up activity.	pencils	30 min.	U6, Les. 1	👤
Citizenship Pages 90–91	**The First Amendment** Children read about the First Amendment and complete a writing activity.	pencils	45 min.	U1, Les. 4	👤

UNIT 5 Planning Options

individual   partners   group/class

	Activity	Materials	🕐	Link	
Drama Activity pages 94–97	**Heroes** Children read a readers theatre play about heroes.		45 min.	U5, Les. 4	
Simulations and Games pages 98–99	**Who Am I?** Children guess heroes from a related item.	large box, pictures or items representing heroes, index cards	20 min.	U5, Les. 4	
	Courage and Caring Children come up with actions related to courage and caring.	butcher paper, beanbags	30 min.	U5	
	Dates in History Children play a matching game with a calendar.	blank calendar pages, black squares of construction paper, pencils	30 min.	U5, Les. 3	
	Immigrant Box Children imagine what it must have been like to be an immigrant.	old suitcase, paper, pencils	30 min.	U5, Les. 2	
Long-Term Project pages 100–101	**Cultural Festival**			U5	
	Week 1 Children are introduced to the project.	paper, pencils	30 min.		
	Week 2 Children choose the country they will study and plan their project.	writing paper, pencils	30 min.		
	Week 3 Children work on the setup for the festival.	supplies to make invitations, materials to set up festival, such as decorations or utensils	60 min.		
	Week 4 Children present their projects.	student-prepared materials	60 min.		

	Activity	Materials	🕐	Link	
Short-Term Projects pages 102–103	**Initial Biographies** Children create autobiographies focusing on culture and traditions.	drawing paper, crayons or markers	30 min.	U5, Les. 3	🧍
	Culture Collage Children create a collage of items that represent American culture.	drawing paper, magazines, newspapers, scissors, glue or tape	30 min.	U5, Les. 2	🧍
	Class Quilt Children create a quilt from portraits.	construction paper, photographs or self-portraits of each child, tape or glue	30 min.	U5, Les. 1	🧍🧍🧍
	Design a Medal Children design a medal for a hero.	examples of medals, pictures of heroes, drawing paper, ribbon or yarn, crayons or markers	30 min.	U5, Les. 4	🧍🧍
Writing Projects pages 104–105	**A Journal Entry** Children write a journal entry.	paper, pencils	30 min.	U5, Les. 2	🧍
	Holiday Traditions Children write about one of their family traditions.	paper, pencils	45 min.	U5, Les. 3	🧍
	Immigrant Interview Children create a list of interview questions.	paper, pencils	15 min.	U5, Les. 2	🧍
	Moving On Children create a list of items they would take with them if they were immigrating.	paper, pencils	30 min.	U5, Les. 2	🧍🧍🧍
	A New Classmate Children write questions about another culture.	paper, pencils	30 min.	U5, Les. 1	🧍🧍🧍
	What's in a Name? Children create a list of locations on a map or globe.	paper, pencils, map or globe	30 min.	U5, Les. 1	🧍🧍
Why Character Counts pages 108–109	**Respect** Children read about respect and complete a follow-up activity.	pencils	30 min.	U5, Les. 2	🧍🧍
Economic Literacy pages 110–111	**Wants and Choices** Children read about wants and choices, and complete a follow-up activity.	pencils	45 min.	U6, Les. 2	🧍
Citizenship pages 112–113	**Rights and Freedoms** Children read about rights and freedoms, and complete a writing activity.	pencils	45 min.		🧍

UNIT

Planning Options

♦ individual   ♦♦ partners   ♦♦♦ group/class

	Activity	Materials	🕐	Link	
Drama Activity pages 116–119	**Rocks of Gold** Children read a readers theatre play about people in the marketplace.		45 min.	U6, Les. 1, 2, 5	♦♦♦
Simulations and Games pages 120–121	**Assembly Line** Children simulate an assembly line for a given toy.	assembled toys (model car, board game, stuffed animal, etc.)	30 min.	U6, Les. 3	♦♦♦
	Trade Charades Children draw and guess countries and products.	index cards	30 min.	U6, Les. 5	♦♦♦
	Shopping Trip Children make a wish list for a shopping trip.		20 min.	U6, Les. 1	♦♦
	I Have, You Want Children review jobs providing services and jobs providing goods.		20 min.	U6, Les. 1	♦♦♦
	Let's Go Shopping Children set up a "store" with school supplies.	labels, classroom objects, play money	30 min.	U6, Les. 1, 5	♦♦♦
	Goods Matching Game Children match producers with the goods they sell.	index cards	30 min.	U6, Les. 1	♦♦♦
Long-Term Project pages 122–123	**Town Shops Model**			U6, Les. 1, 2, 5	♦♦♦
	Week 1 Children brainstorm ideas for an imaginary town.	paper, pencils	30 min.		
	Week 2 Children plan goods, services and advertisements for their store.	paper, pencils, drawing paper, crayons or markers	30 min.		
	Week 3 Children create their store.	small boxes, milk cartons, glue, art supplies, crayons or markers, construction paper	45 min.		
	Week 4 Children present their model town.		30 min.		

	Activity	Materials	🕐	Link	
Short-Term Projects pages 124–125	**Store Graph** Children make a bar graph of items sold in a store.	drawing paper, crayons or markers	45 min.	U6 Les. 1	
	From Factory to You Children research how a factory product is made.	research materials, index cards, string, tape, crayons or markers	45 min.	U6, Les. 3	
	Worldwide Trade Children make a table of imported items in their households.	drawing paper, pencils, crayons or markers	30 min.	U6, Les. 5	
	Produce and Consume Children make a poster showing producers and consumers of a product.	construction paper, mail-order catalogs, crayons or markers, paste, scissors	30 min.	U6, Les. 1	
Writing Projects pages 126–127	**Where Does Money Go?** Children make a book about money.	paper, pencils	30 min.	U6, Les. 2	
	A Good Job for Me Children write about jobs they would like to have when they are adults.	paper, pencils	30 min.	U6, Les. 1	
	Start a Business Children plan a new business.	paper, pencils	30 min.	U6, Les. 2	
	Likeable Labels Children design a package for vegetables.	empty packages of canned, frozen, or fresh vegetables, paper, pencils	30 min.	U6, Les. 3	
	People at Work Children write captions about jobs.	pictures from newspapers and magazines, paper, pencils	30 min.	U6, Les. 1	
	To the Store Children write about transportation.	paper, pencils	15 min.	U6, Les. 5	
Why Character Counts pages 130–131	**Trustworthiness** Students read about trustworthiness and complete a follow-up activity.	pencils	40 min.	U6, Les. 1	
Economic Literacy pages 132–133	**Cost of Goods** Children read about the cost of goods and complete a follow-up activity.	pencils	30 min.	U6, Les. 4	
Citizenship Pages 134–135	**Voting** Children read about voting and complete a writing activity.	pencils	45 min.	U1, Les. 3	

Answer Key

Unit 1
Daily Geography (pp. 18–19)
1. north, east, south, west
2. 50
3. accept appropriate answer
4. west
5. states
6. Arizona, Nevada
7. Wisconsin
8. a capital
9. Minnesota, Iowa
10. Mexico
11. Missouri
12. Washington
13. Pacific Ocean
14. Atlantic Ocean
15. east
16. Michigan
17. El Paso, Texas
18. Austin, Texas
19. San Diego, California
20. New Hampshire, Massachusetts
21. Louisiana, Mississippi, Alabama, possibly Georgia
22. United States of America
23. North America, South America, Africa, Australia, Antarctica, Europe, Asia
24. North America
25. Atlantic, Pacific
26. Asia
27. Pacific
28. Asia
29. east
30. Hawaii

Why Character Counts (p. 20)
when it treats everyone equally

Character Activity (p. 21)
1. Answers will vary. Possible answer: raise your hand before you speak.
2. Answers will vary. Possible answer: make sure the rules treat everyone equally, ask a teacher to help.
3. Answers will vary.

Economic Literacy—Try It (p. 23)
1. Alicia can volunteer as an artist. She can offer to paint a new sign for the city. The city will not have to pay any money to replace the sign.
2. Dr. Walker can offer to check the teeth of the children in families that are very poor. This helps the families because they do not have the money to pay the dentist.

Citizenship (p. 24)
1. It tells how our government is set up and identifies the power each part of the government has.
2. the power to make sure laws are fair

Write About It (p. 25)
Answers will vary but should include an example of cooperation.

Unit 2
Daily Geography (pp. 40–41)
1. a drawing that shows where places are
2. what the map shows
3. map symbols
4. map key
5. compass rose
6. map grid
7. Phoenix
8. Cheyenne
9. Washington, D.C.
10. Virginia and Maryland
11. desert
12. landform
13. border
14. Washington, Idaho, Montana, North Dakota, and Minnesota (also accept Alaska)
15. a model of Earth
16. continents
17. oceans
18. Answers should include four of the following: Alaska, Hawaii, California, Oregon, or Washington.
19. Answers should include four of the following: Maine, New Hampshire, Massachusetts, Rhode Island, Connecticut, New York, New Jersey, Delaware, Maryland, Virginia, North Carolina, South Carolina, Georgia, Florida, Alabama, Mississippi, Louisiana, or Texas.
20. south
21. mountain
22. hill
23. plain
24. Mississippi River
25. Great Lakes
26. equator
27. Antarctica
28. east
29. Pacific Ocean
30. Canada

Why Character Counts (p. 42)

Answers will vary. Answers could include by honoring our country's symbols, saying the Pledge, and singing the national anthem.

Character Activity (p. 43)

Answers will vary.

Economic Literacy—Try It (p. 45)

1. Mr. Owens provides plumbing service. Mrs. Owens provides goods by selling books.
2. Answers will vary.

Citizenship (p. 46)

1. Citizens have the right to own property.
2. Answers will vary. Possible answer: It makes them happy.

Write About It (p. 47)

Answers will vary.

Unit 3

Daily Geography (pp. 62–63)

1. St. Paul
2. Des Moines
3. west
4. Idaho
5. Colorado, Utah, and Nevada
6. Texas and New Mexico
7. West Virginia, Virginia
8. Idaho
9. Columbus
10. Texas
11. city or urban
12. rural or country
13. urban
14. suburb
15. Boston
16. Denver
17. Atlanta (Atlantic Ocean)
18. Lincoln, Nebraska (Abraham Lincoln);
    Madison, Wisconsin (James Madison);
    Jefferson City, Missouri (Thomas Jefferson);
    Jackson, Mississippi (Andrew Jackson)
19. INDIANApolis and OKLAHOMA City
20. east
21. Phoenix, Arizona
22. Denver, Colorado
23. Asia
24. Australia
25. South America
26. south
27. California, Arizona, New Mexico, and Texas
28. Maine
29. Bolivia
30. Beijing

Why Character Counts (p. 64)

Possible response: It means to know when someone is in trouble and to want to help them. It means to help someone who is sick or in trouble.

Character Activity (p. 65)

1. Possible responses may include my parents show care when they pack my lunch or take me fun places.
2. Possible responses may include helping out those in need or not littering.
3. Possible responses may include cheering up someone who is sad; helping them stay safe, helping them figure out the problem; helping them to the nurse's office.

Economic Literacy—Try It (p. 67)

1. make a budget, save money
2. Answers will vary but should show an understanding of budgeting.

Citizenship (p. 68)

1. the same rights
2. color of their skin, religion, where you are from, or whether you are a boy or a girl

Write About It (p. 69)

Answers will vary.

Unit 4

Daily Geography (pp. 84–85)

1. river
2. west
3. Texas
4. Washington and Alaska
5. Pacific Ocean
6. Red River
7. Colorado River
8. Missouri River
9. Salt Lake City, Utah
10. Gulf of Mexico or Atlantic Ocean
11. Florida
12. Salt Lake City, Utah
13. Maryland
14. Albany, New York
15. Minneapolis
16. Huron, Ontario, Michigan, Erie, and Superior
17. St. Paul
18. Colorado and Wyoming
19. Nile (Africa)
20. Mt. Everest (Asia)
21. pipes and sprayers
22. product map
23. climate
24. wet
25. cold
26. dry
27. Portland, Oregon
28. Baton Rouge
29. Ohio River
30. south

Why Character Counts (p. 86)

Answers will vary. Sample answer: It is the responsibility to vote to elect good leaders.

Character Activity (p. 87)
1. Possible responses can include ways children help the teacher or each other, clean up their desks and work areas, do their homework, or be an active part of a group.
2. Possible responses can include that they help classmates when they don't understand or get hurt, they help the teacher put things away or pass out supplies, they help parents by doing their chores, they help siblings by sharing and being respectful.
3. Possible responses can include they follow rules and pick up litter, they conserve resources and recycle, they take care of parks and public areas they use.

Economic Literacy—Try It (p. 89)
1. He is a producer because he sells stuffed animals, games, toy trucks, and dolls, which are all goods. He also wraps toys that are presents as a service.
2. Mrs. Garcia is both a producer and a consumer. Mrs. Garcia's goods are flowers. Her service is delivering the flowers. Mrs. Garcia was a consumer when she bought the dog collar.

Citizenship (p. 90)
1. freedom of speech
2. to talk about what they think is right and wrong

Write About It (p. 91)
Answers will vary but should include mention of freedom of speech and how it can be used to talk about what is wrong.

Unit 5

Daily Geography (pp. 106–107)
1. Colorado
2. Alaska and Hawaii
3. northeast
4. North Carolina
5. Alabama
6. New Hampshire
7. south
8. Arkansas
9. west
10. west and south
11. Oklahoma, Kansas, Nebraska, and South Dakota
12. Nebraska and Iowa
13. Connecticut
14. Asia
15. Africa
16. Pacific
17. Canada
18. Rio Grande
19. Pacific
20. Atlantic
21. North America
22. Indian
23. Australia
24. Asia
25. south
26. east
27. Asia
28. Seattle, Washington
29. San Antonio, Texas
30. Oakland, California

Why Character Counts (p. 108)
It means to be nice to others even when they are different.

Character Activity (p. 109)
Answers will vary.

Economic Literacy—Try It (p. 111)
1. They can go fewer times to the amusement park and use the money they save to help pay for new bikes.
2. Answers will vary but should display understanding of making choices.

Citizenship (p. 112)
1. protection against unfair laws, the right to seek happiness
2. for a better life and more freedom

Write About It (p. 113)
Answers will vary.

Unit 6

Daily Geography (pp. 128–129)
1. Carson City
2. Nebraska
3. Kentucky and Virginia
4. Nebraska (Lincoln)
5. north
6. Missouri
7. east
8. Mississippi
9. ArKANSAS and West VIRGINIA
10. Lake Michigan
11. Georgia and Alabama
12. Santa Fe
13. Oregon and Washington
14. Missouri
15. Atlanta
16. Columbus
17. Sacramento
18. New York, Delaware, Pennsylvania
19. Oahu
20. east
21. Mississippi, Alabama, and Georgia

22. Phoenix
23. Charleston, South Carolina
24. Asia
25. Massachusetts
26. Arizona
27. North America and Europe
28. Australia and Antarctica
29. South America
30. Africa

Why Character Counts (p. 130)

Answers will vary. Sample answers: You tell the truth and follow the rules. You do what you say you will do so people know you mean what you say. You do not take things that are not yours.

Character Activity (p. 131)

1. by giving the wallet to a trusted adult, who can get in touch with the person who lost the wallet
2. Answers will vary. Responses should include examples of how children told the truth, did as they said, or followed the rules.

Economic Literacy—Try It (p. 133)

1. The price will be high because everyone wants one.
2. The price will be lower because fewer people want to buy the car.

Citizenship (p. 134)

1. They vote to choose their leaders, they vote to choose what most of the people want.
2. Possible responses: They must be a U.S. citizen, at least 18 years old, and they must sign up to vote.

Write About It (p. 135)

Stories will vary but should include a vote.